Facebook Marketing Like I'm 5

The Ultimate Beginner's Guide to Mastering Facebook Advertising Tools, Fan Growth Strategies, and Analytics

Peg Samuel, Matthew Capala

Copyright 2015, 2016

No part of this publication may be replicated, redistributed, or given away in any form without the written consent of the author/publisher or the terms relayed to you herein.

Author Photos: Mani Zarrin, Tommy Mendes
Cover Design: Natalie Leeke
Editorial Direction: Stephen C. Baldwin
Research: Tasha Hunter

All Rights Reserved | Zeit Media LLC | "Like I'm 5" is a Registered Trademark

Contents

About the Authors... 10
Foreword... 14
Preface... 16

LET'S BE FRIENDS
Facebook for Business: The Strange Case of Dr. Jekyll and Mr. Hyde... 20
Facebook Myths Debunked... 24
7 Deadly Facebook Sins to Avoid... 28

HOW TO GET YOUR FIRST 1K FANS
Facebook Page Dilemmas... 38
Beginner's Toolbox: Facebook Essentials... 46
Get Your Pretty On: Profile Optimization... 52
How to Attract Your First Facebook Fans... 62
How to Develop a Winning Facebook Strategy... 66
Facebook Strategy Worksheet... 70

THE ROAD FROM 1K to 10K FANS
How to Scale, Pipeline, and Schedule Your Content... 74
Boosting Posts to Get More Eyeballs on Your Content... 86
Advertising on Facebook that Works... 90
Step-By-Step Guide to FB Ad Manager... 92
Understanding Facebook Insights... 104

FACEBOOK LIKE A PRO
Advanced Tools for Brands... 116
Facebook Success Stories... 120
Facebook Custom Audiences... 124
Who to Follow... 130

BONUS
Like I'm 5 Guide to Instagram... 134

Praise for Facebook Marketing Like I'm 5

I regret not reading *Facebook Marketing Like I'm 5* before launching my own book. It packs more value than an MBA class and you can literally use it as a play-by-play to get your 'magic' out to the world. If you're looking to build a strong, authentic, and respected presence, then this book is certainly for you.

Matt Cartagena, Co-author of "Accelerate," Head of Business Development at Grow.co

Facebook Marketing Like I'm 5 is a critical tool for any small business owner who wants to leverage the power of the massively engaged Facebook audience. The chapters are outlined as specific outcomes that any business owner will want (such as "Getting Your First 1K Fans") and then breaking out the process to achieve those goals in an easy step-by-step process that you can do in minutes. Even if you consider yourself a Facebook pro, you'll find tidbits and hacks that will give you a whack on the side of the head.

Ivana Taylor, Small Business Influencer, Publisher at DIY Marketers

Facebook Marketing Like I'm 5 offers more than 'how-to's.' It weaves in the importance of quality content throughout each chapter and provides solid examples of this content.

Kathy Murray, President of Harvard Business Women's Network, Chair of Executive Forum Angels

What I love about what Peg Samuel and Matthew Capala are doing here is that *Facebook Marketing Like I'm 5* is completely actionable and results-oriented. The two are dynamic social media educators and practitioners, which is a rare combination to find. Their natural curiosity means that they tend to figure out what's next with respect to social media ahead of most others – which is exactly what you need to succeed in today's crowded marketplace.

Jeremy Goldman, Author of "Going Social," Founder and CEO at Firebrand Group

Peg and Matthew's book gives a realistic yet optimistic view of how marketers can use Facebook. While many are wringing their hands, worrying over the decline of "reach," Peg and Matt offer clear, straightforward advice and tips on how to use Facebook effectively in today's environment.

Amy Vernon, Adj. Professor at NYU, Social Media, Columnist at Inc Magazine

What I believe to be best thing about this book is how it combines principles, theory, and example in a comprehensive manner. Additionally, the fact that *Facebook Marketing Like I'm 5* directly addresses issues that commonly occur – such as starting, scaling, and maintenance over time – makes it a must read for those looking for help in becoming successful on Facebook.

Gary J. Nix, Chief Strategy Officer and bdot, an integrated branding agency

Hallelujah! Finally a book about Facebook for the 40-something crowd! We're running businesses while racing to understand the social space. This book is the perfect solution. Funny, engaging, relevant, and smart. These authors know how to keep my attention and demystify a very important business tool. Thank you!

Rena DeLevie, Chief Compassion Officer of The Roundtable Business

Facebook Marketing Like I'm 5 is a practical, useful resource for both social media beginners as well as for those who want to brush up on their skills. I put some of Peg and Matt's suggestions into practice immediately.

Shari Rudolph, Senior Marketing Executive, Adjunct Faculty at Irvine Valley College

Facebook Marketing Like I'm 5 is a simple, actionable read with a lot of great insights that drive real results. Matt and Peg did a wonderful job debunking some of the Facebook myths and providing some practical growth strategies that anyone can use to grow their business. If you are using Facebook to grow your business online, this is a must read.

Julbert Abraham, CEO of AGM, "The LinkedIn Guy"

Facebook it still a mystery for many businesses and brands. Peg and Matthew help to unlock all of what Facebook has to offer in a simple and easy way that everyone can understand. *Facebook Marketing Like I'm 5* will help you move to the next level with your Facebook marketing. 'Cause if you're not using Facebook, you're not really doing business.

Mike Street, Social Media Strategist at Burrell Communications

Peg and Matt have created one of the most practical, to-the-point Facebook marketing guides for businesses out there. It covers most of the biggest headaches of Facebook marketing that business owners may encounter, and offers a clear plan of attack to best utilize the channel. One of the "must reads!"

Mike Le, COO at CBI Digital

Social media marketing is no longer a nice-to-have channel; it's a necessity. And the landscape is always changing. One player that's here for the long haul is Facebook. Matt and Peg do an excellent job of highlighting the keys to success in *Facebook Marketing Like I'm 5*. Whether you're a newbie or a seasoned marketer, you're guaranteed to take away valuable insights from this easy to read guide.

Lara Nicotra, Marketing Manager at 16 Handles

Facebook marketing can be a challenge for brands without full-time support teams, but Matthew and Peg take what's hard and make it simple. This book will kick-start your Facebook strategy to provide real value to your brand and give you actionable tips on day one. In an age when everyone is on Facebook, it's not enough to be present; you also have to be excellent. *Facebook Marketing Like I'm 5* will get you there!

Chad G. Abbott, Partner at Abbson Studios

Facebook Marketing Like I'm 5 is a valuable guide, which breaks down what Facebook has to offer into an easy-to-understand format for brands and entrepreneurs. Whether you're looking to jumpstart your social media strategy – or refine your current strategy – you've come to the right place.

Amelia Tran, Social Strategist at Firebrand Group

Social Media marketing is king and Facebook is an unquestionable centerpiece. Knowing how to rule that kingdom is crucial and Peg Samuel has given us the key, opened the door, and provided a comprehensive guided tour and battle plan on how to rule it. Matthew Capala's additions give the extra yet bullseye-accurate intel that supercharges anyone's arsenal. A must read and must-have tool for any business owner – even if you think you already know it all.

Marc Raco, Host of Fashion Is Your Business and Executive Producer of The Hope Is Project

The best approach to social media marketing written to date. It reads like an operations manual written in simple English. If you want to refresh your approach to marketing on Facebook, reading this should be your standard protocol.

Marc L. Van Valen, Co-Founder and CEO at Digital Cloud Designs, Inc.

If you ever thought that you couldn't get a handle on Facebook marketing, this book will change everything.

Adam Connell, Founder of Blogging Wizard

Facebook Marketing Like I'm 5 is one of the best Facebook resources out there. If you're new to social media and want to use it to make an impact with your customers, this book is for you. The book provides real-life examples with brands and companies we all know and love on what to do and what *not* to do. Easy to follow instructions on everything from engaging with customers, merging pages, content scheduling, branding, and more!

Sarah Dunn, Co-host of the We Live Limitless

Being competitive on Facebook is not as simple as many people think. *Facebook Marketing Like I'm 5* digs into all the little pieces necessary to build a solid Facebook presence, breaking them down into easy-to-follow steps and worksheets. Matthew and Peg give us key takeaways that are spot-on and proven by the real world examples included throughout the book.

BJ Smith, E-commerce Coach and Podcast Host of The Busy Marketer

Facebook is much more complex than it use to be. *Facebook Marketing Like I'm 5*, an essential guide for beginners and experts, provides insight and easy tactics to navigate the Facebook landscape. The information brought me up to speed very quickly on how to generate more leads for recruitment for our employer brand. It really helped me get the most out of Facebook — I was able to overcome some challenges and achieve our business goals.

Sonya Magett, Talent Brand Manager at Game Show Network

Marketing on Facebook may be daunting to many, but it isn't rocket science, and so it's fantastic to see a book on Facebook marketing that's completely free of NASA-style jargon. What most business people and entrepreneurs need—and what *Facebook Marketing Like I'm 5* delivers—is a clear, up-to-date, results-driven guide that won't overwhelm them, letting them instead focus on the concrete tactical actions required to improve performance on the world's largest social network.

Stephen C. Baldwin, Author of "NetSlaves: True Tales of Working the Web"

Wow. If you've ever wondered how to use Facebook strategically but haven't been able to find a good resource to give you a roadmap for success, look no further. This book is for you. Matthew and Peg hit it out of the park with *Facebook Marketing Like I'm 5*. It really is THE complete book on how to go from beginner to great with your Facebook Marketing. Highly recommend.

Ryan Rhoten, Personal Brand Management Coach, Host of the Brand New You

I usually tell clients that social media can be waste of time, but what I mean is it's a waste of time if you're doing it wrong: without thought or strategy. Now, instead I'll tell them *Read Facebook Like I'm 5*, which cuts through the social media BS and gives clear and actionable information that will greatly enhance their marketing.

Pia Silva, Partner at Worstofall Design

Haters love to hate, but the truth is that Facebook's still where everybody (and their mom) hangs out. So embrace it. Peg and Matthew break it down into a handy manual, answering all of the practical questions you've been wondering. But they don't leave out the "why" driving their instructions and advice, so that *Facebook Marketing Like I'm 5* speaks to both the smart beginner and the marketing expert who maybe just needed to get back in touch with the nitty gritty.

Leiti Hsu, Food Show Host of WORD OF MOUTH on Heritage Radio Network

Straightforward and very practical advice for succeeding at Facebook marketing. There's something for everyone, no matter what level of skill you currently have. Heavy emphasis on advertising, which is crucial for success on social.

Mark Walker, Founder of Punch Bag Marketing

This book packs a punch! Peg and Matt delivered! Oh my goodness. I've only been reading this book for a day, and I already have actionable how-to's to take back to my clients.

Sarah Weise, UX Director at Booz Allen Hamilton

About the Authors

Peg Samuel

Peg Samuel, Adjunct Professor at New York University and Founder of Social Diva Media; she is a proven leader in online brand building and digital strategy. With twenty years experience in the digital marketing arena, Peg turned her love of communications into a lucrative and insight-driven Social Media consultancy specializing in social media strategy, brand influencer campaigns, and execution marketing for lifestyle, luxury, and high-profile celebrity brands.

Peg has worked with media brands including W Hotels, Harper's Bazaar, InStyle, and Vogue. Other special projects include the NBC Olympics Games (known as the first "Social" Olympics), the 55th Annual GRAMMY Awards, and the New Music Seminar. Peg is a sought after speaker, she has been on panels and given talks at Social Media Week, WIX, Social Media Breakfast, Internet Week New York, and Digital Hollywood.

Peg is the author of "*How to be a Social Diva*;" she's also produced two music albums with International House's music label, Strictly Rhythm: "Strictly Social Diva." She has received attention from E! News, MSNBC, Entrepreneur Magazine, and Good Morning New York. Her social networking contact base reads like a Who's Who in the entertainment, media, and advertising industries.

Useful Links:
Website: http://socialdivamedia.com/
Facebook: https://www.facebook.com/socialdiva
Twitter: https://twitter.com/socialdiva

Matthew Capala

Matthew Capala is the President of Alphametic, an organic growth accelerator specializing in SEO and social media workshops, with a portfolio of worldwide brands including L'Oreal, Hoval, and Quest Diagnostics. As a prolific Internet entrepreneur, Matthew has built several popular blogs, including Search Decoder and Sumo Hacks. He is a sought-after International speaker and trainer.

His work and ideas have been recognized by Mashable, Chicago Tribune, and The Huffington Post. As Adjunct Professor at NYU, Matthew teaches a course on search marketing and social media analytics. He writes regularly on The Next Web and is the author of four books, including *"SEO Like I'm 5: The Ultimate Beginner's Guide to Search Engine Optimization."*

With over a decade of digital marketing experience working with some of the world's largest brands (Apple, Western Union, Smirnoff, Dell, LG, and Prudential) and emerging startups, Matthew has leveraged the Internet in unprecedented ways to spur growth. Formerly Head of Search and Inbound Marketing (the Americas) at Profero (later acquired by Lowe & Partners), Matthew has built a million-dollar business, growing the group from one to nine in less than two years. Former leadership positions include specialist roles at Mindshare, Mediacom, Zeta Interactive, Mattel, and The Associated Press.

Useful links:
Website: http://alphametic.com/
SEO Blog: http://www.searchdecoder.com/
Life Hacking Blog: http://sumohacks.com/
FB: https://www.facebook.com/matt.capala/
Twitter: https://twitter.com/SearchDecoder

Other Books by the Authors

Peg Samuel

How to Be a Social Diva, An Essential Guide for the Girl About Town

Matthew Capala

SEO Like I'm 5: The Ultimate Beginner's Guide to Search Engine Optimization

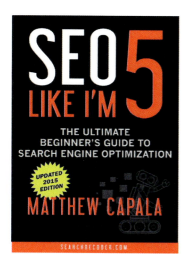

Soloprenuer Ronin: Break the Chains, Earn Your Freedom, and Engineer a Happy Internet Lifestyle Blogging From Anywhere

99 SEO Tools for 99 Cents (Kindle Only)

Foreword

"Facebook marketing is dead." "Organic reach is gone." "There's no point in your business spending money on Facebook."

Oh, really?

What's fascinating to me is how much invalid information is out there about Facebook as a marketing tool. It's actually getting to the point of ridiculousness, but it remains nonetheless.

Part of the reason is that many pundits look to make a name for themselves by gravitating toward new platforms rather than acknowledging all the benefits of staying with a stalwart like Facebook.

Facebook has a proven track record of modernizing itself for over a decade now. From Facebook insights to ad manager to custom audiences and much more, there's so much functionality for businesses to take advantage of. But they don't.

"Facebook Marketing Like I'm 5" is a great starting point for navigating all the options available for businesses and entrepreneurs. If you are looking to outfox your competition and become profitable on the largest social network in the world, you've come to the right place.

Plenty of how-to books fall victim to the trap of appealing to either very early beginners or to the highly advanced crowd, in which case their appeal is pretty limited. Facebook Marketing Like I'm 5 is approachable for beginners, but will also appeal to those with a level of marketing and/or technical sophistication, but are looking for a Facebook deep-dive.

What I love about what Peg Samuel and Matthew Capala are doing here is that "Facebook Marketing Like I'm 5" is completely actionable and results-oriented. The two are dynamic social media educators and practitioners, which is a rare combination to find. Their natural curiosity means that they tend to figure out what's next with respect to social media ahead of most others – which is exactly what you need to succeed in today's crowded marketplace.

I look forward to seeing you – and your businesses – on Facebook!

Jeremy Goldman, Author of "Going Social: Excite Customers, Generate Buzz, and Energize Your Brand with the Power of Social Media," Founder and CEO at Firebrand Group

Preface

Make no mistake; this is no 'Facebook for dummies.' We wrote 'Facebook Marketing Like I'm 5" to serve as the ultimate social media training system for businesses and entrepreneurs who are *smart beginners*.

This is a practical book. Our goal is to give you an actionable roadmap for a total makeover of your Facebook business strategy that will increase your audience growth and deliver real business results.

Because you can't succeed in social media marketing without a strategy, Facebook Marketing Like I'm 5' takes you through the strategic process of planning and building a Facebook business presence. You will learn how to attract new customers through a magnetic Facebook community built around your own unique brand of content. You'll also learn how to gather not just Likes - but *the right kind of Likes* - that can move your business ahead and bring you profits and more market share.

This book also covers the all-important tools you'll need to execute your strategy. 'Facebook Marketing Like I'm 5' features dozens of these free tools; step-by-step guides; 'under-the-hood' tricks, real-world case studies, and examples of successful (and not so successful) campaigns from brands both big and small.

What you'll learn

There's an overload of information about Facebook scattered across the web. Some of it is out of date, and much of it is confusing, overly granular, or vague.

'Facebook Marketing Like I'm 5' is built around an action-oriented, workshop-style, pain-free process to plan, build, and optimize your Facebook business presence.

This book will show you how to:

- Choose the right Facebook settings for your business
- Use actionable worksheets and templates to develop and execute your Facebook marketing plan

- Choose which free marketing plugins, apps, and CTAs to use
- Optimize your Facebook profile and content
- Boost your organic engagement
- Identify the right advertising tools for your business
- Build targeted user profiles
- Use Facebook's Ad Manager
- Attract fans to your content
- Get new Likes and convert them into leads
- Track and measure success
- Use Facebook Custom Audiences for hyper-targeting and remarketing
- Avoid common Facebook marketing mistakes and pitfalls

Who is this book for?

- Business owners
- Entrepreneurs and startups
- Brands and corporations
- Celebrities, authors, artists, public personalities
- Bloggers
- Marketing and social media professionals
- Students

We know that Facebook marketing takes thought and work, but that doesn't mean that you can't have fun while you're doing it. So we strove to make this book as easy to understand as possible by including plenty of screenshots, templates, worksheets, and step-by-step instructions you can use while reading it.

Let's Be Friends

Think about what people are doing on Facebook today. They're keeping up with their friends and family, but they're also building an image and identity for themselves, which in a sense is their brand. They're connecting with the audience that they want to connect to. It's almost a disadvantage if you're not on it now.

Mark Zuckerberg, CEO of Facebook

Facebook for Business: the Strange Case of Dr. Jekyll and Mr. Hyde

Mark Zuckerberg is a nice fellow. But when he remarks that "it's almost a disadvantage" not to be on Facebook, he's guilty of gross understatement. (We'd argue that any business trying to grow today without having a Facebook presence is *definitely* disadvantaging itself.)

The real problem, however, is that Facebook isn't a very friendly marketing environment (despite Facebook's own claims to the contrary). In fact, we'd go so far as to say that Facebook presents two very different personas to the marketer: a nice *Dr. Jekyll* side and a quite scary *Mr. Hyde* side.

"The Strange Case of Dr. Jekyll and Mr. Hyde" is the original title of a novella written by Robert Louis Stevenson that was first published in 1886. It is about a London lawyer who investigates strange occurrences between his old friend, Dr. Henry Jekyll, and the evil Edward Hyde. It has become a part of the modern language, with the very phrase "Jekyll and Hyde" coming to mean a person who is vastly different in moral character from one situation to the next.

The Dr. Jekyll side is Facebook's "sunny" persona – engaging social network with billions of users, excellent analytics and marketing tools, plus an ultra-easy self-serve model that makes it possible to spend just a few dollars – perhaps $10 to $25 a day – to move your business forward.

Facebook's darker, more malicious "Mr. Hyde" side was only revealed recently. This side brutally forces you to "pay to play" using its ad system, or face invisibility trying to communicate with your fans and followers organically.

The grisly death of Facebook organic reach

It wasn't always so bad. Once upon a time – as recently as two years ago – getting your message out on Facebook organically was easy and inexpensive. Facebook worked a bit like the Web: even if you didn't pay a toll, your content would still be visible, in other words, you enjoyed some measure of "organic reach."

Organic reach was something that brands took for granted because they thought they'd earned it. After all, hadn't they put Facebook's big blue icon on their TV, print, transit and billboard ads? Weren't they helping Facebook (which makes no content of its own) when their teams cranked out content for the service each day? Hadn't brands earned a right to distribute their wonderful branded content using Facebook's free pipes?

No they hadn't.

In November, 2014, Facebook lowered the boom on brand content and what it called overly "promotional" posts, when it announced on its official blog that:

According to people we surveyed, there are some consistent traits that make organic posts feel too promotional:

- Posts that solely push people to buy a product or install an app
- Posts that push people to enter promotions and sweepstakes with no real context
- Posts that reuse the exact same content from ads

Beginning in January 2015, people will see less of this type of content in their News Feeds.

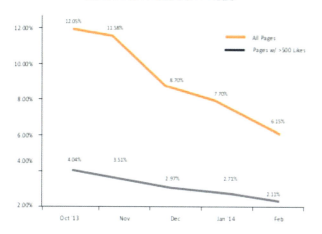

And so it was done. Marketers – bad ones and good ones alike – saw their organic reaches shrink to a fraction of their former selves. Subsequent research by Ogilvy reported that "large brands' Facebook posts reached just 2% of their fans (a number that was falling by .5% per month).

More research by Forrester showed that on average, only .07% of top brands' Facebook fans interact with each of their posts."

Here's a terrifying account from a marketer whose organic reach was gutted by the algorithm change:

We have spent countless thousands of dollars with FB advertising and got ourselves to the point of having 145,000 fans and now we have been SLAPPED in the face by FB... PRIOR to July 1st, when we posted content we could expect 3000-6000 views on the post with our 145,000 fans... Suddenly, July 1st hit and our post views fell into the black hole/abyss. Now we are averaging 135 (NO I'M NOT JOKING! 135 people to MAYBE 400 if we are extremely LUCKY... are seeing our posts)... With the click of a few buttons and changes to your algorithms on 7/1/14 you are essentially crippling my method of making a living and supporting my family.

Taking Facebook's Jekyll/Good along with the Hyde/Bad

If there's a silver lining in Facebook's rampage against promotional posts, it's this: it drove many "huckster-style" marketers away from Facebook, creating more space for smart marketers to reach out using less intrusive tactics. Second, Facebook has introduced various advertising tools, with reach and targeting capabilities unmatched by any other social network.

But there's no question that the algorithm change made it more difficult – for every brand lacking an unlimited social media budget – to break through without buying clicks.

Facebook's change didn't obviate the need for marketers to build compelling pages, create high-quality content, or otherwise engage with the service in an organic way. Free, organic visibility is still important on Facebook.

But it added a new burden: the necessity to buy eyeballs – in as efficient and targeted a way as possible – or yield ground to competitors and become irrelevant.

In today's media environment, invisibility is a fate much worse than failure for any business large or small.

We'll teach you specifically about buying eyeballs effectively with Facebook's advertising tools in a later chapter. Right now, however, let's talk about avoiding the common mistakes that marketers make on the platform. These mistakes are usually driven by an unconscious acceptance of certain damaging myths about marketing on Facebook.

So let's go demolish some.

5 Facebook Myths Debunked

Avoiding mistakes on Facebook starts with debunking some major myths.

Let's start with the big one:

Myth #1: More posts equals more likes

Although consistent posting is important (all social algorithms reward volume), what matters more is the success of your effort to provide actual value – not just volume – to your followers and fans. Two principles apply here: "pay it forward" and "less is more." "Pay it forward" in a Facebook context means stepping forward and offering some kind of resource, service, or business that the world needs. The "less is more" principle applies too because posting too often, or posting uninteresting, irrelevant content, is the top reason that people will unlike your page and shut you out of their conversations.

Be thoughtful. Be careful. As a brand or branded individual, success means sending out interesting, authentic, relevant content on a regular basis. Then and only then will you accumulate public approval in the form of "Likes" and other positive behaviors.

Myth #2: Everyone sees my posts

Once upon a time, this statement might have been true. But as we discussed earlier, Facebook has massively reduced the "organic reach" of brands to encourage more use of its advertising platform. People are sometimes shocked to hear that only 1 percent of their fans will see any of their posts unless they're "boosted" (paid for). But that's today's reality, and you're going to have work in within it if you want to build a sustainable presence on Facebook.

Myth #3: Set it and forget it

Social media networks thrive on actual human activity. Don't make the mistake of believing that you can "set and forget" your Facebook presence. Yes, you can automate your posts (we'll show you how to do this in a subsequent chapter), but you can't walk away for days or weeks at a time and expect anything other than moss to grow on your page. Today, Facebook rewards brands that respond, and respond quickly, to consumers and prospects with a chance to display a "Very responsive to messages" badge on their profiles. This telegraphs to users the fact that the business is active, responsive, and ready to conduct business. You should strive to be one of those "very responsive" brands to earn maximum trust and traffic: consider it an official Facebook "seal of approval" for your efforts.

Myth #4: Build it and they will come

Facebook is a marketing channel and you'll need to work to integrate it with any other marketing channels you're using. Once your page is launched, its URL needs to be listed in all of your marketing materials, linked to from your website, and installed in your email template. The most successful businesses are the ones that best integrate their social channels with their pre-existing marketing channels, creating a seamless experience among them – the result is a much faster-growing fan base.

Myth #5: Engage! It's social media

Ok that's not a myth. In fact, it's a MUST DO. Social media thrives on community and two-way conversations. To create any kind of high-quality, authentic dialogue, you must ENGAGE with your audience. Think about it: would you call someone on the phone, dump a bunch of info on them, and then hang up? Of course not.

Reply in a timely manner to people who are engaged with you on social media; doing this proves that there's a human being in the loop who cares and is there to help. Stay on top of your calendar and post frequently (but not too much). Regularly engage with your followers – as a human being – if you want to get any real human results.

Need more incentive to regularly engage? It comes directly from Facebook, because when you engage with one of your posts, the post is redisplayed in the news feed – both for your own followers and the feed of the person with whom you're engaging. When it goes back into the feed like this, it means more eyeballs will be on your post, with potential for greater reach and "virality." This means FREE marketing.

Key Takeaways:

- Create interesting, authentic content
- Start to think about boosting posts
- Make a calendar and keep up with your content
- Market your page on your other marketing channels
- Engage

7 Deadly Sins for Your Brand's Facebook Marketing

Before we get into the nuts and bolts of building your Facebook business presence, let's imagine that you've gotten your brand up and running on the biggest, most recognized, most powerful social media site in the world. You've read the articles, the tips, the advice. You've got savvy young interns and experienced content management teams working hard to make sure your brand reaches your audience. Or you're doing it yourself as a bootstrapping solopreneur.

But hold on a second. Before you hit that "Post" button, did you know that what might sound like a small slip-up to you – a typo, a misplaced photo, a poor hashtag choice – has cost some of the biggest brands in the world millions in lost revenue?

On average, companies can expect to lose about $4.3 million in global sales because of social media mistakes. Those who don't pay attention to the details can confuse and frustrate their followers on a massive scale. A small mistake can easily snowball into an error with huge consequences.

Here are 7 of the biggest Facebook blunders made by some of the most highly-regarded brands in the world. We want to serve them up to you early, so you don't make the same mistakes!

Talking like a robot

Apparently, Domino's Pizza isn't used to getting compliments. When a customer posted a compliment on the fast food giant's Facebook page, the brand replied with an automated apology, "So sorry about that! Please share some additional information with us and please mention reference# 1409193 so we can have this addressed."

The brand's failure to use a human voice turned an opportunity for a positive customer interaction into an embarrassing moment that was then massively amplified via social media.

Don't use robo-posts. Social media is a conversation and replies must be human and authentic. While marketing automation has a role to play in terms of gaining efficiencies and capturing metrics, it should never be viewed as a replacement for true human interaction.

#Going #HashtagCrazy

It's an ongoing question – to use hashtags on Facebook or not? By analyzing 200,000 Facebook posts, Social Bakers found the optimal number of hashtags to be between 1-2. Using more hashtags than this can cause a significant drop in interactions. And let's face it, "hashtag-stuffing" makes your company look desperate for attention and Likes.

Starbucks is on the wrong side of this research and its hashtag-happy approach puts it in danger of lowering engagement with its fans. Stick to 1 or 2 relevant hashtags - in Starbuck's case, "strawsome" is unique, clever and all they need.

Big Dog Manufactured Homes
3 Dog Manufactured Homes

Take the above advice or the only hashtag your brand will be found under will be #youredoingitwrong!

Deleting posts

If you want your fans to abandon you as quickly as possible, go ahead and delete their messages from your Facebook areas. When people took to Smuckers' Facebook to criticize its stance on GMO labeling or ask questions about GMOs in their products, Smuckers casually deleted the posts and pretended they never existed. When the website GMOInside.org learned of Smucker's "strategy," they wrote their own posts to Smuckers, which were promptly deleted as well.

The questions were an opportunity for Smuckers to elaborate on its stance and respond to customer feedback. By simply speaking up instead of bulk deleting questions, a lot of the negative backlash could have been managed before things get out of hand.

Being boring or overly "salesy"

Today's consumers are tired of the same old companies doing the same old kind of advertising; more than half of Facebook users have unfollowed a brand for being too salesy, self-praising, or boring.

GM is a prime example of a huge brand that is unfortunately using Facebook to blandly broadcast to its followers, rather than engaging with them. Don't take my word for it; here's an example:

Don't be like GM and treat your fans as if they're unwilling participants in a quarterly sales meeting. Customers want to relate to the companies they do business with and they're open to seeing what makes that company unique and different.

Forgetting that content is global

The day before the Swedes took on Portugal in a crucial World Cup qualifier, Pepsi Max ran a series of ads on their Official Facebook page in Sweden. The ads featured Portugal's soccer superstar, Cristiano Ronaldo, as a voodoo doll caught in a variety of unfavorable positions (such as lying prone on a railroad track).

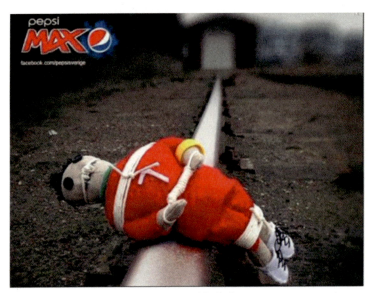

Normally, the rest of the world wouldn't have sees an ad created in Sweden, but the Portuguese were offended and let the whole world know it. A Portuguese anti-Pepsi Facebook group managed to build 100,000+ fans in a single day, and Pepsi was forced to pull the ads and issue an apology (it's not known what happened to their ad agency but I imagine it wasn't good).

Learn from this costly mistake – even if you don't think of your company as a global entity, you must remember that everything on the Internet is seen everywhere.

Making bad jokes

7-Eleven thought they had a pretty good sense of humor when they decided to share a Facebook comment referencing Mental Health Month.

While some fans likely found this post funny, most found it offensive and 7-Eleven was forced to learn a social media strategy lesson the hard way. The blowback from their poor decision was harsh and quick and put the company in a very unfavorable light for quite a while. If your company wants to tie into a holiday or event, you'd better make sure you "dot your i's and cross your t's" and not mistake insult for humor. You don't want to be that guy.

Looking for shortcuts

Begging is never pretty, not under any circumstances. Asking for Likes on Facebook is digital begging at its worst and says, "we don't have a strategy and we're not even sure who we are" better than any press release could. Oxiclean is the poster child for this social media taboo. Not only did they blatantly ask for Likes, but they weirdly combined the request with tax filing season.

No, I don't get it either. I just know you probably shouldn't have either of these components in your marketing strategy. Don't beg or buy fans... earn them with solid strategies and engagement.

Getting Started

So there you have it. Sure, there are many more than 7 mistakes to avoid when it comes to branding and Facebook, but if you can steer clear of these deadly ones, you'll be on your way to more fans and more customers.

How to Get Your First 1K Fans

Congratulations! Any toxic myths about marketing on Facebook should now be debunked, and you should now be able to avoid the worst mistakes that marketers make on Facebook. This puts you in the 95th percentile of social marketers.

Now let's get to the serious business of building your presence on Facebook, growing your network, and starting to drive meaningful business results.

Facebook Page Dilemmas

When launching a business Facebook page for the first time, you will likely have many questions. Don't worry: you're not alone; many of our clients come to us with big questions about this issue. Frequently asked questions include:

"Should I start a fresh fan page?"

"Do I keep both a fan page and a personal page?

"What if I am a Public Personality and have 5,000 friends?"

"Should I post the same content to both pages?"

We've even been asked "should an author launch a page for each book she writes?"

Are you any of these people? We've got an answer for you. The bottom line is this: whether you're a Public Figure or are a representative of a business, you want a Facebook business page for your enterprise. Why? Because a business page lets you access juicy tools like analytics, post boosts, ads, and more.

Apply the K.I.S.S. principle

It's best to observe the K.I.S.S. ("keep it simple, stupid") principle on Facebook. It's not a great idea to launch too many business pages. Think about it: it's more confusing, more time-consuming, there's more for you to keep up with, and your fans will become fragmented and dispersed across too many pages.

If you've made too many pages and want to get things under control, stick with us, because we're going to show you how to merge them.

Say what?

If you have several pages, then you've got to come up with content for each or you will be posting the same thing in several places. Conversely, your fans won't always have access to all of your communications in one place.

Does this describe your situation? It's a mess, right?

Here's a far better approach, using the example of our friend Gabby Bernstein, a New York Times author.

As of today, Gabby has four books, she lectures all over the world, she has a video series, and we know she is currently writing book number five. Imagine if she had a Facebook page for every book, product, project launch, etc. All of this would be way too much to keep up with! Instead, she has one – and only one – page where her fans can conveniently find out all about her latest projects and events.

Take a close look at the screenshot below. You'll notice that Gabby has included all of her projects in one spot. The genius of including it all is that fans who visit the page for one thing can then be surprised and delighted by all her other offerings.

Consolidate!

Lots of people make the mistake of launching separate pages for different aspects of their professional lives (I know I did). But the idea today is to have all of your fans in the same place. This way, you – and your audience – spend more time on one page instead of spreading themselves thin across multiple pages.

How can you do this?

Merge your pages. Facebook now has a handy tool that lets you do this. The process of asking for merging is simple (then the Facebook gods decide if the pages are enough of a match to merge). There are rules around merging, for example the rule holding that the content and the title of the page need to be very similar – we'll talk about these rules shortly.

Step-by-step guide

Let's look at an example from Peg's brand. Here's how she merged two pages – the first one being an old page that had accumulated 368 Likes – with the new one that she wants to serve as her new conversational hub on Facebook. (The page was created to support her first book, *How to be a Social Diva,* back in 2009. It was completely separate from her business page).

Merging pages combines all of your fan Likes and check-ins into one page. You will need to be the admin of both pages to do so.

To merge your pages:

- Go to Facebook.com/pages/merge.
- Select the page you want to keep from the first drop-down menu, then select the page you want to merge from the second drop-down menu.
- If your pages can be merged, click Merge Pages.

You might get a screen saying "Facebook cannot merge, the names are not similar." If you think they are similar enough, go ahead and keep clicking; it will ask you again.

It takes seven days to merge pages; Facebook will send you a series of updates letting you know the status. In this seven-day period, Facebook will let all fans of the first page know that it's going to be merged into the new one.

You can check on the status of the merge at any time in your "page support area."

But I'm already a Star!

What's the best way to leverage one's personal network for the good of one's business?

There are several approaches: you can utilize your friends to market your business (we'll talk about this in the How to Develop a Winning Facebook Strategy chapter). Or – if you've got over 5,000 friends and want to turn these people into fans of your business – you can request that Facebook change your personal profile to a Public Personality page. Your friends will then become your fans, but be careful: this process will cause all of your posts to be deleted. Make sure you backup this information first if it's important to keep a record of these posts

Backup, baby!

Download your post information from your Facebook settings page. To download this information:

- Click at the top right of any Facebook page and select "Settings"
- Click "Download a Copy of Your Facebook Data" below your "General Account Settings"
- Click "Start My Archive"

Because this download contains your profile information, you should keep it secure and be careful when storing, sending, or uploading it to any other services. Facebook only gives you 24 hours to save any backups. File them away and keep them in a safe place.

Shhhhhh!

What do you do if you're a Public Figure and people keep trying to "friend" you instead of liking your page?

If you're trying to keep your personal profile well... personal, then you can change your name so it's not searchable. For example, you could use your first and middle name, an inconspicuous alias, or you could even make up a nickname for yourself. This way, fans won't find you but you can still find your friends. (They'll know, trust us.)

Matt has used this approach with his personal page. If you look for Matthew Capala you'll only find his "Business Person" page, but go ahead and try to find his personal page. He's clever right?

Key Takeaways

- Launch a Facebook Business Page
- Utilize only one page for all of your business projects, products, and events
- Keep your personal and business pages separate
  Merge to remove redundant pages (but back up post data first)

Beginner's Toolbox: Facebook Essentials

If you're a newbie to Facebook and Facebook business pages, there's a fair amount of "lingo" you'll need to learn. This short list of basic terms will help you "speak Facebook" and be better able to navigate your way through Facebook's marketing system:

Facebook Dictionary

Timeline - The timeline (formally known known as the "wall") is the column on Facebook that shows all of your posts, arranged in reverse chronological (newest first) order.

Posts - Are the copy, comments, pictures, and/or videos you post or schedule to be posted to your Timeline.

Business Page - This is the traditional "Like" page. When we refer to Personal Brands or Public Figure profiles, it's their Business Pages we'll be referencing throughout this book.

Personal Page - A personal page is what you set up in Facebook to "friend" your friends, relatives, kids, parents, and colleagues. We will not be focusing on your personal page in this eBook; we'll be focusing on Facebook "business pages."

Profile/Icon Picture - This is the small 180 x 180 pixel picture that shows up on both your Facebook page and as a smaller "thumbnail" icon in the news feed.

Cover Photo – When looking at your page, this is the larger picture that sits above and behind your profile picture

Boosting - Whenever you post something, you have the option to "boost it," which means paying Facebook money in order for more people to see it. "Boosting" is synonymous with advertising on Facebook.

Ads - The advertising platform for Facebook.

Tabs - Next to your profile picture, there are text entries displaying "Timeline", "About," "Photos," etc. These are known as Tabs and you'll want to set them up correctly. We'll tell you how to do this in the Get Your Pretty On: Profile Optimization chapter.

The "Feed" - When you post a status update or any type of content to Facebook, the information will also be displayed to some of the people who are following you in their "news feeds."

Now that we've got your Facebook vocabulary set, let's dive deeper.

Picking the right Facebook URL

The first thing you want to do is pick a clear title for your brand or your personal brand. Usually your actual brand name will be perfect. For your personal brand, your name is the best choice. You also want your URL to be easy, so it is searchable.

Here are two examples of URLs that are short, clear, and consistent with their brand names.

https://www.facebook.com/Lifeisgood
https://www.facebook.com/FreePeople

About

When you click on the "About" section, you will see a list of basic information to fill out.

Pick your category. For example, are you an educational business? A consulting firm? Personal brand? The category you pick will show up next to the business profile icon on your cover photo.

In this example, you can see that the fashion brand Free People has selected "Clothing" as a category, and this choice represents their brand clearly and simply.

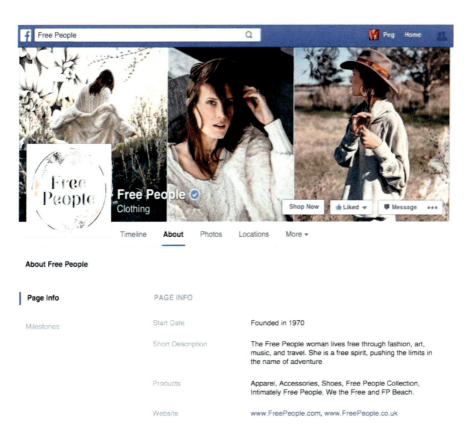

You can edit your web address in this area; again you want it to be consistent with your business name so it will be easy for people to find your business.

Make sure to enter sub categories so people can use Facebook's search functionality to find your business.

Describe Your Business

You now have the opportunity to write a short description – and a more discursive, long description – about your business.

Your short description should be clean and concise, and be identical to the description used on any other social networks you use. When writing your 'About' section, we recommend using the same keywords someone would put into Google to discover your brand. (Discovering the keywords that tell your business story comes from using Keyword Research Tools (Google Keyword Planner, Google Trends, and 3rd party tools like Moz). If you need help, Matt's book, SEO Like I'm 5, provides all the details.)

Make sure you include your website URL in the description. (It's just one more way for people to visit your website and – if you've set up your site to convert them – become a real customer.)

Does your business have a physical location? If so, add it here. Doing so may provide a way for people to "check in" when they visit. (We'll have more to say about how the "check in" process provides you some free marketing oomph a bit later).

Finally, you can add your mission statement, products, phone number, email address here.

The About area is also the place where you are assigned a Facebook Page ID. We will talk about this later.

Tabs

Tabs are the sections displayed across the top of the page, below your cover photo and above your timeline. The basic tabs are About, Photos, and Videos. You can customize this area and add entries for your other social networks. These will also be displayed on the left hand side of your page.

Here's a screenshot from Peg's business page. Notice that the "more" button includes all of her tabs, including Twitter, Videos, Pinterest, Instagram, etc.

Facebook Plug Ins

After you've set up your page, you can arrange to have your other social networks link to it. This doesn't mean that you're going to be posting content from these other networks to your timeline: what we want you to do is use plug ins that will appear as separate tabs.

An easy FREE way to do this is with https://woobox.com/

If any of this seems overwhelming, don't let it get to you. You can go back at any time and edit, change, complete, or remove the information you've added to your page.

Key Takeaways

- Ensure everything is crystal clear
- Choose appropriate Name, URL, Descriptions, and Categories
- Use Woobox plug in to bring in your other social networks
- Make sure Page Info area is completely filled in

Get Your Pretty On: Profile Optimization

When it comes to your Facebook business page, the cover skin and photo you choose are extremely important; having them here is like waving a "we're open for business" sign. Your cover photo needs to be powerful, appealing, and relatable. Adding some simple text to a great image can make all the difference.

Brand yourself

First impressions are important. When people visit your Facebook page, they'll decide in seconds whether to stick around, take the actions you want, or click onto something else. As a business owner or personal brand, make sure your page looks professional and polished. Consider your Facebook page to be an extension of your other digital brand efforts. Stay consistent across all platforms and be mindful of the best practices on Facebook.

When setting up your brand page cover photo, here are things to take into consideration about the choices you'll need to make.

Let's look at some examples:

One of Peg's favorite bands, Magic Giant, is a fun folk revival band that always displays top-notch pictures. Their cover photo below is interesting, well lit, and represents their brand's three members in a fun way.

If you're using text in the cover photo, make sure you consider the layout this text will live on top of. For example, while we both love U2, check out the weird effect that their cover photo produces within the default formatting of the Facebook layout. Although clever in that it promotes their album, notice how the image-based text is covered up by Facebook's own text. This doesn't look good at all.

Let's look at a better treatment. Here you'll see how our Fight Song friend Rachel Platten used best practices when she designed her cover photo. It's spot on. She's considered the formatting, her image is clear and well lit, the Facebook text sits well above the profile info and she's also promoting her product. Way to go, Rachel!

Facebook Cover Photo branding tips

Your Facebook cover photo is not only your storefront; it's another opportunity to market yourself, your products, or services. So make the most of it.

Here are some examples:

Rachel is a smart marketer. How do we know this? She's promoting her album on her cover photo, and also – in the description. Notice how she's inserted links to purchase it.

In the cover photo below, notice that Peg is not only promoting her online school, but she's also keeping it on-brand, alluding to her logo by using the same shape and color in both images.

It's always a good idea to fill out the description for your cover photo. This gives you some extra marketing potential. In Peg's example, she has included some marketing copy promoting her school, supported by a link to click through to buy.

Always use your cover photo as a marketing tool. Your cover photo is not only a visual representation of your brand or business: it's another opportunity to do real marketing on Facebook by driving behavior.

Here's another fact about the cover photo that merits your attention: whenever you replace it with a new cover photo, news of this change ripples out graphically through the news feeds of yourself and others, gaining it additional visibility at no cost to you. So even if you're cover photo is "perfect," it's good to change it every so often (perhaps once every two weeks).

CTAs (Calls to Action)

Back to Peg's cover page. Notice that she's also optimized the "sign up" button, which can be changed at any time.

Let's take a closer look at how Peg did this. When clicking the sign-up CTA button as an administrator, you'll see the following:

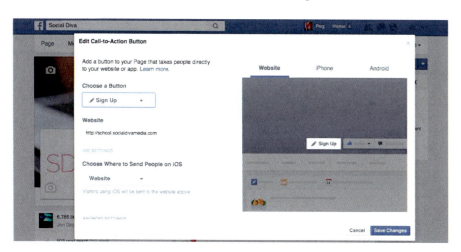

Here, you can edit links and or change the kind of promotion displayed on the Cover Photo page.

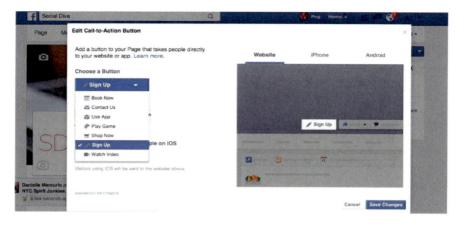

Notice all of the options available to you to use. They include:

- Sign Up
- Book Now
- Contact Us
- Use App
- Play Game
- Shop Now
- Watch Video

These CTAs can be supplemented with Facebook apps, which can be inserted right into the page tab area. There are hundreds of useful (and not so useful) Facebook apps you can add to your page.

Some of our favorites marketing app types include:

- Email capture apps (including popular email provider Mailchimp).
- RSS apps (so updates from your website appear right on the page)
- Social Media integration apps (so updates from other services appear on your Facebook page.
- Contest apps.
- E-commerce apps that effectively embed a commerce platform within Facebook.
- Poll apps that let you tap into the sentiments of your audience.

3rd party apps are great, and you should experiment with them. But such apps tend to come and go on Facebook, so it's good to think about whether you can get by with Facebook's pre-built CTAs. The advantage of going with Facebook-built software is that you can be sure that it will be kept up to date and trouble-free.

Tips

- Think about changing the cover photo every month
- Update it when you have a special promotion or offer
- Keep it visually appealing
- Remember Facebook formatting defaults
- Use CTAs and apps to drive specific behavior on your Page

You can

- Draw inspiration from seasonal events
- Promote products or services
- Announce new programs or events

What about the Icon or Profile Pic?

Now we're talking about the smaller box (where the arrow points to in the screenshot below).

Best Practices

- Have a consistent icon on all social media networks
- Size of icon is 180 x 180 to 160 x 160 (1:1 aspect ratio)
- We recommend using a graphical icon (as opposed to simply using text)

Should you use your logo or a picture? Well, that depends on whether you're a business or a personal brand. For businesses, we recommend a logo that will be visually appealing given the limited dimensions available. For personal brands, use a professional picture and make sure this picture is appealing, even when displayed in the small-format thumbnail size displayed in feeds.

Make sure you utilize the description area for your icon in the same way you did for your cover photo; doing so provides another chance to market your business.

Labeling Your Page

If you're starting a new business page, there are a lot of options available for labelling.

Here are a few examples of such labelling:

- Musician/Band
- Public Figure
- Food/Cooking
- Charity Organization
- Product/Service

When it comes to labeling your page, ensure that what you offer as a product or service is clear. For example, for the brand Casper (showed here), there is no question about what the page and brand is about.

DIY Tools

Some great resources for creating beautiful Facebook-worthy images:

- Canva
- PicMonkey
- Photoshop

Final Takeaways

- Maintain clear, consistent branding on both your Cover Photo and Icon
- Ensure that all images provide additional marketing opportunities, including your cover photo
- Utilize the CTA (Call to Action) button for your business
- Keep your messaging professional and impactful

How to Attract Your First Fans

Your page is live and it looks great. Now the question becomes "how do you get people to find it?"

Don't take it for granted that people will just show up on their own. To reach audiences interested in what you do, you have to find where these people live in the groups, channels, and streams on Facebook.

Think about your new page the same way you do about your website.

You have to market it. That begins with leveraging your strongest asset: your pre-existing social network: the people who are already part of your personal and professional life.

Leverage Your Network

One of the handy tools Facebook gives you is an "Invite Friends to Like this Page" button.

Check out this screenshot of Peg's Social Diva page. When you click on this button, it will pull up all of your known friends.

Be Strategic About Who You Invite

It's OK to invite your mom, some pals, and other personal members of your tribe to Like your business page. But your main drive is to build a fan base that is relevant to your brand. Pick only those friends and family members whom you believe would really be interested in your content and your business.

Tell Everyone! (Email Siggys and More)

Today, people have been conditioned - by TV ads, billboards, even icons on trucks and trains - to believe that every business has a Facebook page. So your existing customers or potential customers will assume you're there too.

Make it super easy for them to find you.

Put it on your business card, link it from your website, include a link on your email template, announce it to your email database, if you have a physical location place a poster at your POS (Point of Sale). The opportunities to promote are endless, so be creative and encourage people to Like your page and share with their friends.

Buying Likes

You've probably heard about fake Likes.

Hundreds of sites offer this service. Here's a promotional testimonial from one such "fake Like" service:

"With the additional Facebook likes through your site I was able to reach more clients and drive the business further…without having to invest copious amounts of my own time reaching out to people. Overnight my Facebook 'likes' sky-rocketed after using your service. I am more than impressed!. It delivers results fast. Well done!" - J L

We doubt this is true, there is no silver bullet don't let these types of claims fool you.

You never ever, ever want to buy fans.

Let us repeat it: *never.* Why?

First, they fakeness negates any value to for your business. They will never be engaged or buy from you.

Second, they are a liability to you. Facebook knows exactly who's accessing its network, and is aware of the fake Like phenomenon. It can and will scrape and block fake Likes and this could happen at any time. One day you'll look like "a big shot" and the next day your numbers will fall to zero.

This is not a good look. It's also a PR disaster in waiting if somebody important (perhaps tipped off by one of your competitors), suggests your fast-growing audience is imaginary.

The fake Like industry only exists because social media services have done a bad job of distinguishing real from robotic behavior. As they get better, this industry will wither.

True, people still buy fake Likes, but people do risky, stupid things every day, and that's zero reason to emulate them.

Final Takeaways

- Market your page to your friends
- Be strategic about who you invite
- Include an icon in your email and on your website
- Include in your email signature
- Never buy fake Likes

Developing a Winning Facebook Strategy

Merely having a Facebook page is not enough. We don't subscribe to the "build it and they will come" philosophy because we've never seen it work. If you really want your Facebook page to work for your business, you need to put thought into what your Facebook strategy will be and come up with a bulletproof plan. Having a clear plan will work in your favor and save you time when you're creating your content and devising a publishing calendar.

After you have launched your new business Facebook page, then the real work begins.

Four Pillars of Building Your Facebook Strategy

1. Promoting and utilizing the page
2. Your target market
3. Advertising and promoting your page
4. Content

Think about your Facebook page as a microsite offering unlimited opportunity for traffic. How do you harness the power of the billions of people on the platform for your better business good? We're going to tell you how.

Promoting and Utilizing

Think through how you want to promote and utilize your page. Revisit your business goals for having a Facebook page. Which one of the following goals applies?

- Selling products
- App downloads
- Brick & mortar traffic
- Selling services
- Promoting events

Your Target Market

Next, think about who exactly who you're targeting. Who is your perfect customer? When you're thinking about your targeting, the "demographic" of your target speaks to its age, gender, and location. You'll also need to think about the "psychographics" of your target audience, such as personality, interests, values, and lifestyles.

What other brands, services, and companies do they Like?

As an example, say you specialize in female yoga clothing. You could potentially say, "my target market is any woman that does yoga," but targeting in this kind of broad manner makes it difficult to market effectively.

Think about it. You wouldn't speak to a 20-something in the same way you would to a 40-year old to get your brand message across, would you? The same applies to messaging and imagery: there are many brands on the market that essentially sell the same product, yet the way they present their branding is designed to resonate very differently with different target demographics.

Think about your digital voice and how it will effectively speak to your ideal follower, and then craft your content accordingly.

What if you have more than one target market?

That's OK. Most companies do have more than one audience. First, identify the audience segment that's most lucrative for you. What do your most profitable customers look Like in terms of demographics, psychographics, or online behavior? Develop a model of this audience: it will be your primary audience; other less valuable but still important groups will become your secondary audiences.

Let's take the yoga brand example again.

You've got your primary audience; say it's 30-45 year olds that like yoga. You also may want to target yoga instructors (because lots of yoga students see them and look at their outfits). Therefore, yoga instructors would be your secondary audience.

Some questions to ask yourself when identifying your specific customers are:

- What is the age range I'm trying to reach?
- How much money do they make?
- What do they do in their spare time?
- How do they Like to get their information?

Some brands will write out a whole description about the "persona" they are trying to reach. For example, "Meet Jennifer! She lives in NYC, likes to run on the West Side Highway path, she enjoys a hard workout. She eats Paleo, not vegan. She goes by the motto 'work hard, play hard.' She is busy; you probably won't find her at the Farmers market... "

Homing in on "who" you are trying to reach will help you immensely when you want to speak to them.

When you write out the copy to accompany any post picture or video, you'll always want to think about how you're getting your message across to the specific groups you've identified.

Here's an example from the brand lululemon athletica:

Here's another example, from the Life is Good brand. This includes a strong Call to Action:

Content

Content is serious business. If your content sucks, so will your results. Period. You've got to think about user experience. As we always say in the digital world: "content is king." Content – whether it's text content or visual content – needs to be relevant, compelling and timely. Think about how can you add value (knowledge, insight, utility, benefit) to your target customer.

For example, if you were to visit the yoga clothing company page, it might offer value by providing information about quality fibers, where they're sourced from, and why they're chosen to make such a high-quality garment. Along with the information, you'll want to have a great picture or perhaps a cool edited "behind the scenes" video of these garments being planned and made.

Final takeaways

- Have clear business goals for your Facebook business page
- Get specific on your primary and secondary audience
- Think about how are you marketing your page
- Think about the valuable content you'll be offering

Facebook Worksheet

Here's a worksheet that we give away in our online school to help you along. We've consulted hundreds of business using this tried-and-proven system. Take a few moments to fill it out. Doing this now will help you focus your efforts on the strategies and tactics most likely to move your business ahead.

How to Deliver VALUE

If you were to offer 4 kinds of content, what would they be?

1. _____
_____

2. _____
_____

3. _____
_____

4. _____
_____

How are you adding value?

_____
_____

_____
_____

_____
_____

What are you offering?

_____
_____

_____

_____

Any events coming up?

_____

_____

_____

What announcements would you make?

_____

_____

_____

What insider peeks can you share?

(e.g. "behind the scenes" industry insights)

_____

_____

_____

After this worksheet is completed, we ask our students to take an oath: ***I promise I will offer quality content over quantity***

The Road From 1K to 10K Fans

Congratulations again. You've now got a brilliant, compelling business page, have a firm grasp of strategy, and are growing your fan base into the 4-digit zone. Now it's time to accelerate the pace – of publishing, fan acquisition, and your own business growth. It's time to "scale up" (as the entrepreneurs put it) so let's dive right into tactics and strategies essential to making this happen!

How to Scale, Schedule, and Pipeline Your Content

This is usually the time when a lot of clients come to us for help, because they've become frustrated that their page – even though it's great – isn't getting the traction they believe it deserves.

They typically have a ton of questions that you probably have too, such as:

- What will I be talking about with my fans?
- What's the right time to post?
- How often should I post?
- When and where should I promote my page?
- When will I get to 10k fans?

These are big questions but don't be overwhelmed. We're here to tell you that social media is not as challenging as you think. Just plan and take things step-by-step.

Step 1: Content

When you're just starting off with Facebook, the idea of coming up with a steady flow of content worthy of pleasing your audience can seem daunting.

Don't panic. Step away from your keyboard, iPhone, or Android. Take a deep breath. Think about what your potential customer wants to hear — how often, and when.

We'd like to save you time and anxiety by instilling in you the "Less is More" principle mentioned earlier. It holds that a slow or moderate flow of high-quality content will always trump a fast flow of low-quality content (trust us – we've tried both methods).

Quality always beats Quantity on social media. If you understand this basic rule, you'll always run ahead of the pack without feeling like you're on a grueling content treadmill.

The "so what?" factor

When you think about what you want to say to your customers – or potential customers – think about what they want to hear. Put yourself in their shoes. Understand their pain points and problems. What kind of information would help them out?

Peg talks about this a lot in her *Media Relations: Present and Future* NYU class. She presses her students to think about what it is that is actually newsworthy. Why would a media outlet care about what their client is doing?

Think of your content in the same way. What is it that you think your primary and secondary audience wants to hear? Why would anyone be interested in what you're planning to publish? What value does it bring to the discussion?

Here are some ideas for posts that will hopefully drive value for your audience on Facebook.

- News or Information posts. Have you learned something new about an industry trend that would be of interest to others? Is your business the source of information about a new product or service your audience should try? Do you have access to special data (perhaps it's data from your own study) that would be interest to others?

- Do you have an offline or online event coming up? Who's going to be there? Why is this a "can't miss" event?

- Do you have a valuable offer or promotion for your readers?

- Can you give your audience an insider peek into your industry? People love "behind the scenes" access.

Evergreen Content

"Evergreen" content is a term derived from the world of journalism. It's a form of content whose value doesn't decrease as rapidly as news-oriented content does. Evergreen posts aren't time sensitive. They'll work well if they're posted today, tomorrow, next week, of next month.

You'll want to have a fair share of evergreen content in your content plan. Developing a reserve of this high-value, time-insensitive content gives you confidence and flexibility. (Having such a reserve also spares you from the panic that can come when you have nothing ready to post on a given day!)

The most efficient scenario for creating evergreen content entails producing a bunch of content in advance that you can utilize at any time.

Here's an example of evergreen content from Peg's business page. The post is informational, timely, but doesn't have a pressing end date to it. Although the post was published on May 22, 2015, it could just as easily work today, or a month from now. That's evergreen.

Evergreen content is valuable content that can be used at anytime. It's helpful for building out your calendar. It's also nice to have content that can be moved to another date in your calendar if you have an important campaign to run or want to cover a breaking news story.

Campaign Content

When we talk about "campaign content," we're talking about something that has a specific start and end date. It could be notices about a special promotion, a sale, an upcoming online or offline event, book signing, etc.

You'll want this content to work cohesively with all of your other content. Let's use one of Peg's campaigns as an example. This campaign is for a webinar. Webinars are live online events, and Peg's promoting one – with a start and an end date – in the screenshot below.

Here's another example of a campaign from Peg's page. This one has a softer end date (it's for a new product). We'd still consider it a "campaign" since there is a marketing cycle that would go around this new product launch.

Breaking News

Evergreen content and campaign content are essential content types, but you should also strive to mix in news content, especially if you have unique "insider" insights about special areas of your business. Being able to cover breaking news positions you as a brand that's "in the know" and "up on things."

What's breaking news for your business?

- Breaking news in your field
- Press coverage of your business or industry
- Top trends
- Content you provide to other sites

Think about it: when news breaks, people are tuned in, engaged, and hungry to hear the latest developments. Some industries – for example, fashion and entertainment – are heavily driven by news. Others industries might seem sleepier, but only on surface inspection. If you dig even a little bit into these "quiet" industries, you'll usually find raging passions, noisy personalities, and pressing issues.

By paying attention to the news in your business niche and posting content referencing and/or commenting on it, your brand stays relevant. You'll position yourself as an influencer and/or expert. Additionally, any press you receive about your business flows naturally into a well-curated news feed.

One article = many posts

When you publish a single article – to Facebook, your own blog, or another social media platform – you've created one very important instance of this content.

But you're not done. To make the most of our intellectual property, it's best to create "content around this content" that's native to each service you use. You can do this by highlighting the different points made in a single article, perhaps by lifting out quotes, tips, or other high-value information items, and making each the kernel for a new post.

Here's an example from Peg's Page. In this case, Peg had written an article for Whalebone Magazine: *6 Ways to Not Suck on Instagram.*

As you see from these examples, many different posts resulted from the contents of the original article.

Here, Peg's team pulled a blurb out of the piece, thus obviating the need to create any new content for the post. The post was published and tagged, crediting the news outlet where Peg's article was located. Tagging the source not only gives more credibility, it potentially creates more traction for the post.

It's all in the details

Keep your posts short in length. For Facebook, you have a nanosecond to make a claim to someone's attention before they scroll past your post, so limit any text you write in the post to between 2 to 3 sentences.

Always post with a picture or image

Facebook's Edgerank software weighs posts with images more heavily than it does text-only posts. Statistically, such posts perform better and have more potential for people to see them. Plus, being visual provides more opportunities to visually brand yourself. If you're posting about a product or service, people are more inclined to develop an emotional connection if there's a strong visual aspect in play.

Post consistently but don't overpost!

Remember what we said before: 28% of people on Facebook unfollow pages due to excessive posting. Don't let that unfollowed page be yours!

Step 2: Editorial Calendar

Create an editorial calendar, preferably a week to a month ahead. With this in hand, you'll communicate important information on a daily basis that supports your content and informs your readers.

Let's break it down...

Post 3-5 times a week. Start with 3 posts; once your following grows above 5,000, you can increase this to 5 times per week.

If there's an upcoming special event and you are posting several times a day about it, the best practice is to space these posts at least 4 hours apart. (If, however, a news item breaks, you should feel free to add additional posts at will.)

If you have several photos from an event that happened on a single day, it's best to put these photos into their own album.

Make sure your posts are timely, however don't over post. Remember, the "so what" factor.

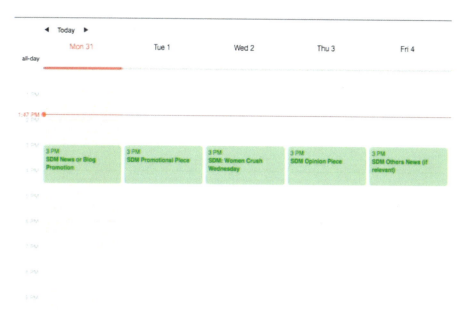

Step 3: Schedule It

Use Facebook's scheduling tool to set up your string of posts for the future. Set up your posts days, weeks, or even months in advance.

Yes, we're aware that there are other scheduling tools such as TweetDeck, HootSuite and Buffer, that can handle post scheduling on Facebook. But there's some evidence that Facebook's Edgerank* software prefers it when you use Facebook to schedule posts, and obviously, you want to ensure every post you publish has the highest potential visibility possible.

Click on the arrow by "Publish," then click on "Schedule"

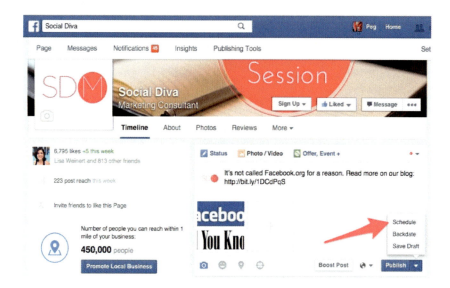

Pick a date and time for your post to publish, and hit "Schedule"

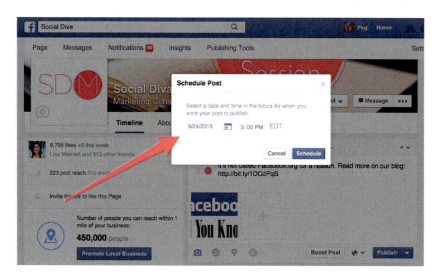

You're all set!

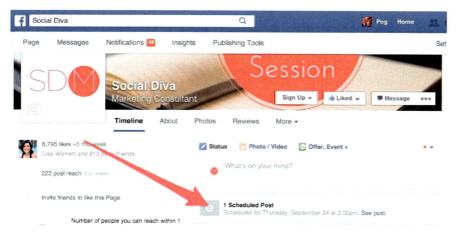

Step 4: Engagement

So far, you've learned about how to think about your content, plan it, and schedule it. But this isn't the time to "set it and forget it." All of this preparation and advance work is to allow you to spend your time on engagement. Remember: you're in a two-way conversation. It's SOCIAL Media.

You must engage. Period.

Getting ready for this new – and hopefully most rewarding – phase of your social media journey begins very simply: with the correct setting of your notifications.

Set your notifications so you'll quickly know when someone is engaging on your page. Doing this is critical, because engagement happens in real time. Even if you don't have time to monitor engagement on a real-time basis, you should check in regularly. Set aside at least two times a day when you check your page for engagement. Response on the same business day is preferred.

Engaging your audience is key to success on social media. Social media is all about you being your authentic brand voice and reaching out to your followers on a regular basis. If you can think of it as simply a regular part of your routine, it will be effortless and fun.

Key Takeaways

- Create authentic, valuable content
- Editorial calendar – Evergreen + campaign
- Never publish a post lacking an image
- Use Facebook scheduler
- Engage with your followers

Implemented in 2010, the Facebook news feed algorithm Edgerank picks and chooses what Facebook users see in their News Feeds. - Source Sprout Social http://sproutsocial.com/insights/facebook-news-feed-algorithm-guide/

Boosting Posts to Get More Eyeballs on Your Content

You've got killer content, it's scheduled, and you're now actively engaging. Yes! You're doing everything we suggested doing in the prior chapter.

Now let's take it to the next level.

How? BOOST your posts.

You've spent all of this time getting it right. Now we're going to help you get more eyeballs on it all.

Facebook makes boosting super simple.

Step 1: Boosting Post

There's a button underneath each of your posts that says "Boost Post"

Step 2: Audience, Location, Budget and Duration

Next a window opens with your first group of targeting options. Up first is:

Audience

In terms of audience, your choices are:

a) People who (already) Like your Page.

b) People who Like your Page and their friends: this is our favorite targeting option because you'll have the chance to hit your target market along with their friends (who are likely to share many similar qualities). Think of this choice as a "blend" of a boost and a regular ad campaign.

c) People you choose through targeting/selected people segmented according to different demographic variables. We recommend you reserve this choice for an actual ad campaign. (We'll cover this in the next chapter).

Of the choices above, we will generally choose "a" or "b" By choosing "a," more of your fans will actually see your great content. By choosing "b," these fans – and their friends – – will see it. This is a slick way to gain more exposure for your existing posts – a blended approach for boosting plus an "extra" degree of outreach.

Location

Select the geographical location where you want your post to be shown. You can choose a national area (such as the entire United States as shown in the screenshot below), or a more tightly targeted area such as a local state or city. Think about which geo areas are relevant to your business goals. For example if you're a local brick and mortar storefront based in Brooklyn, New York, you likely won't want people outside of the New York area to see your post. But if you're an online e-commerce brand that ships nationwide, don't limit yourself to a specific locale.

Budget

Select your budget. Facebook has an automatic setting that you can simply change to meet your needs. The amount you choose depends on what your marketing budget entails. For example, for a small business, we'd suggest a $250-300 monthly ad budget, plus another $100 to boost posts. If you have $100 per month to boost posts, you can decide if you want to spread it evenly – for example, by trying it once a week – or waiting until you have something that is really important to promote. Or a mix of each.

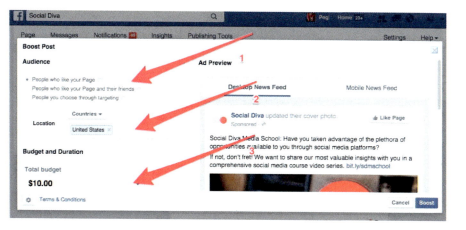

Duration

As you can see in the screenshot below, you can select "1 day," "7 days," or "14 days" and can also choose an end date for the boosted post to stop showing. If you choose "1 day," your post will have more volume on that day vs. the 14 days it would otherwise spread across.

Estimated People Reached

If you change the budget, duration, or location, the "Est. People Reached" number will change. Obviously, more reach is better, but work within your budget. Trust us: you will see results.

Key Takeaway

Remember that Facebook is Facebook.com, not Facebook.org. Visibility on this network isn't free and without a marketing budget, your content won't be seen by more than a tiny fraction of your audience. If you budget is modest (and most are), it's vital to spend strategically.

Advertising on Facebook That Works

We're huge fans of Facebook Advertising. Why? Because it's a highly targeted way to purposefully gain the attention of your desired demographic with guaranteed visibility. You don't have to have deep pockets to have an impact with your ad campaign. When executed correctly, the return on investment can be very real.

Targeting

Facebook is an incredibly powerful platform through which you can market your page to potential new fans based on geographical targeting, demographics, interests, behaviors, other brand page Likes, and even on their friendships with your current fans.

Results

Besides using your page to obtain more targeted Likes, you can utilize Facebook Ads to meet the following objectives:

- Boosting your posts
- Increasing website traffic and conversions*
- Increasing app installs
- Increasing engagement in your app
- Raising attendance at an event
- Getting people to claim your offer
- More video views
- More sales

*You can track conversions directly from your website if you've set up a mechanism to do so. Typically, a pixel is set up on your site's "Thank You" page or within your shopping cart page. This pixel will send a message back to Facebook and populate your reports with data about which ad(s) are performing the best.

You can also set up a "Custom Audience" campaign that targets your own website traffic to turn those people into fans, a point we'll discuss in detail in our "Custom Audiences" chapter. Crafty right?

Step-By-Step Guide to Ad Manager

Using Facebook's ad platform to market your business is smart. Facebook's targeting capabilities are state of the art, offering you many opportunities to break through the Facebook noise. Facebook is always updating Ad Manager. When we wrote this book in late 2015 the latest update had been released, and we like it more than ever.

Also, let's be completely honest here: advertising on Facebook is the only way to reach about 98 percent of your audience. So let's show you how to run an ad campaign using Facebook's advertising system.

Step 1: Select "Create Campaign"

Create your campaign based on any of the following objectives:

- Boost your posts
- Promote your page
- Send people to your website
- Increase conversions on your website
- Get installs of your app
- Increase engagement of your app
- Reach people near your business
- Raise attendance for event
- Get video views

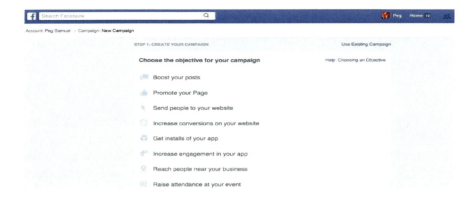

Facebook has many different ways to use its ad platform to drive results for you. For this example, we'll choose "Promote Your Page," an objective which will translate to more page Likes.

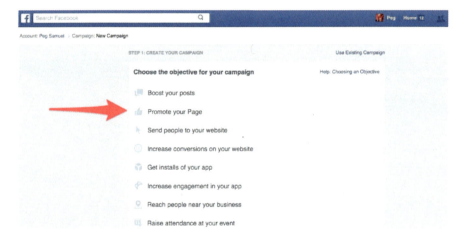

Now choose which page you're promoting (if you're managing more than one), and then name your campaign. Use a campaign title that's as descriptive as possible Here you'll see that Peg chose "Social Diva," then named her campaign "Social Diva – Page Likes FL5". A simple campaign title like this will allow you (or your team) to know exactly what the campaign is targeting.

Step 2: Target Audience

Facebook ads should be shown to specific groups of highly engaged people. By now, you should know your target audience in depth (especially if you did our exercise in the "How to Design a Winning Facebook Strategy" chapter). Use this information to inform your ad targeting decisions.

The top targeting options include:

Location: Any city, country
Demographics: Age, gender, education, and more
Interest: Hobbies, pages they like
Behaviors: Based on purchase behaviors connected to Facebook
Connections: Fans of your page
Current customers: Target email list
Lookalike audience: People similar to those who Like your page

This image is a snapshot of Peg's default audience targeting page:

Fill in the New Campaign area with information describing the appropriate audience for the campaign:

Choose Interests

The "interests" section of Facebook's ad system is very robust and granular. Here Peg can pick people that are interested in "Social Media Optimization, Industry/Digital Marketing." She can even opt for people that Like other top marketers who address these issues such as Gary Vaynerchuk or Amy Porterfield.

Choose Connections

Because, in this example, the objective is more page Likes, it's best to exclude the people who've already Liked the page.

Potential Reach

This area will show you how many people within the audience you've chosen can potentially see your ad. Our suggestion is to have at a reach of at least 25,000 when putting together a set of ads.

Review Audience

This area will let you review the results of your targeting selections.

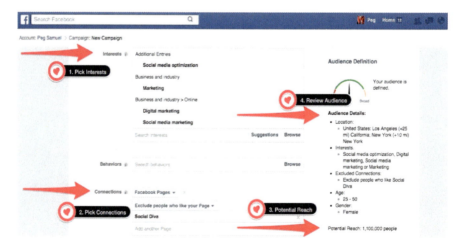

Step 3: Budget, time of day, duration

Set your budget, when you want your ads to run, and for how long. You can set up a campaign to be continuous, or – if you have an end date (such as a launch or an event) – you can schedule your ads to finish on that date and at a specific time.

Below is the default view of Peg's campaign. Make sure that you do the following:

- Set your daily budget.
- Optimize for page Likes.
- Pricing – we suggest "Get the most Likes for the best price." This will allow Facebook to do the optimizing for you.
- Ad Scheduling – because Peg is running in two time zones, and her target audience might be online at anytime, we would let this be "anytime."
- Delivery Type – Standard.

On the right, you can see the Estimated Daily Reach panel. The number in this panel will automatically adjust itself, depending on how much budget is selected over what period of time and which targeting settings are used.

Step 4: Select your images

Before you get into selecting the elements (or "creative") that will go into your ads,, we want to fill you in on some Facebook ad rules and best practices.

Ad Rules

Ads may only contain 20% text in the image (including logos and slogans). You can check to make sure your ad abides by this rule by going to this link: https://www.facebook.com/ads/tools/text_overlay

Ads must be appropriate for the age group targeted.

Ads may not display nonexistent functions (such as "play" or "close" buttons that don't work as described).

Creating Multiple Ads

Each image you add will create a different ad in your ad set. When your campaign starts, you can monitor how audiences respond to the different images and adjust your campaigns accordingly. This is a great way to optimize your campaign like a pro.

Recommended Image Size

1200 x 444 pixels is the recommended size for ad creative. It's best if your ad is already sized when it goes to Facebook; if it isn't, you can crop it within the tool. However if you build your ads with the proper dimensions from get go, they will always upload exactly as you planned with no surprises.

You can use free tools such as Canva and PicMonkey to help you size Facebook ads.

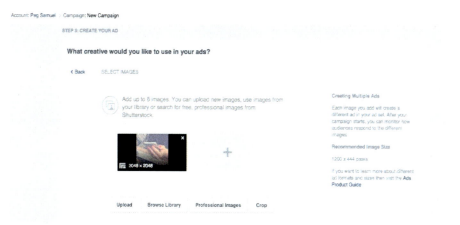

Step 5: Launch

Are you are ready? Click on "Place Order."

After you hit the green button to place your order, your ad will go into a review process for a few hours (Facebook's standard review period is 24 hours). Keep this time delay in mind when you plan to run time-sensitive campaigns.

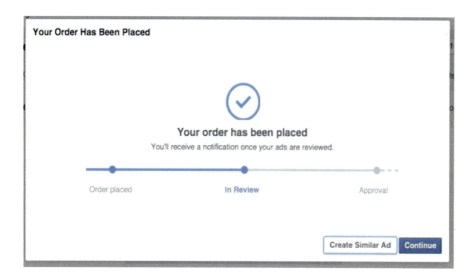

Optimization

We recommend that you launch your campaign with several different creative assets (images) running at the same time. This way, you can double down on ads that are working and turn off or spend less on ads that are not.

There are several ways you can set up your ads to determine what will work best for your chosen objective. First, you can set up ads for Desktop, Desktop Right (which will place ads in the right hand column of the desktop display), and Mobile.

Each ad will look a little different, because formatting will alter sizes and change how the copy is laid out. Clearly mark your ad campaigns so it's easy to tell which one is which.

We also recommend trying several images. The trick here is to keep the copy consistent against the varying images, so you'll know that it is the image – and not the copy – that you need to change. Alternatively, if you're experimenting with different copy, do so with the same image for the very same reason.

This is important: never test more than two variables (image a. vs. image b., or copy a. vs. copy b.) at the same time. Run an image test, choose a winner; then run a copy test, choosing another winner. This process is called "A/B" or "split" testing and it's a proven method for finding winning performers.

For an example of how this works, we'll again look at Peg's page. She knows from experience that that her "Women Mobile" ad placement performs the best, so that's the target she'll use for all of her campaigns moving forward.

Let's look at Peg's live campaign, which she's given about a week to catch on.

We are going to click on her campaign "Social Diva – Page Likes – FL5"

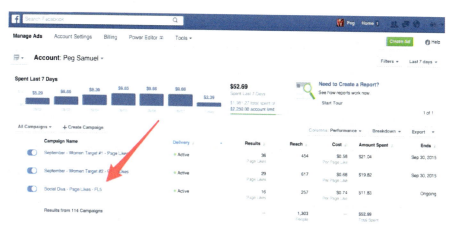

Clicking takes us to her "FL5- Los Angeles, New York – 25-50" ad set. Here we see overall she has a cost of $0.74 per page Like.

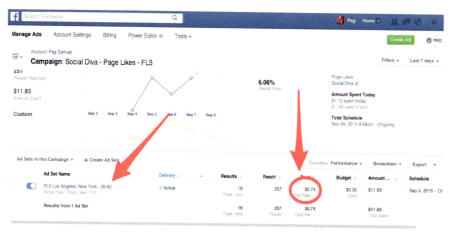

If we click a little deeper, we can look at both the "results" column and the "cost column." In the cost column, you can see that Peg is paying just $0.18 per page Like for ads with Image 1 – that's a lot cheaper than the $0.74 paid for ads with Image 2! So Peg will now turn off Image 2 ads, which lets her double down on the better-performing ads using Image 1.

Conversion Tracking

When there's a specific action you want people to take – such as visiting your website or signing up for your newsletter – you can set up Facebook conversion tracking on your website. This will allow you to understand the real ROI of each and every one of your Facebook ad campaigns.

Doing this means adding a short section of code (known as a "conversion pixel" to your web pages. While this sounds complicated, it's actually fast and easy. From Ads Manager, click on Tools and Select Conversion Traffic. A window will pop up:

Select the kind of conversion event you want to track, and click on "Create Pixel." Now copy the code that pops up into your web site and you'll be able to directly track ROI.

Key Takeaways

- Utilize Facebook Ad Manager for your business Page
- Set up separate targeted campaigns so you can optimize
- Set up several creative assets so you can optimize
- Test your campaigns, drop underperforming ad creative, and double down on winning creative
- Only test 2 campaign variables at the same time
- Add the Facebook Conversion pixel to your site to track ROI

Understanding Facebook Insights

So, you've done all of this work on your page, you've identified your target audience, you're pushing out content, people are seeing your page and your posts.

But how do you know it's all working? And how can you change things to make them work better?

Facebook has a free measurement tool called "Insights" that will give you these answers. You can click on it right from the top bar of your business page:

Once inside the "Insights" area, different tabs reveal different ways to look at your results, including:

- Overview
- Likes
- Reach
- Visits

- Posts
- People

Let's take a look at Peg's Social Diva page to see how this all works.

The Overview tab shows a date range. Within it, you'll find Page Likes (Total Page Likes and New Page Likes).

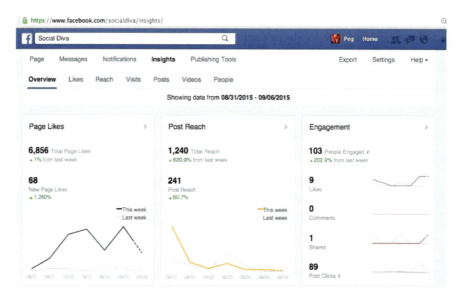

When we click on Likes, we've seen an overview of Likes in their many forms.

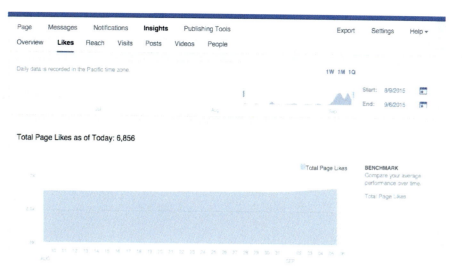

The following screenshot shows "Net Likes," plus a chart for Unlikes, Organic Likes, and Paid Likes. You can even scroll over the info to see exactly what happened on a certain day. For example, in the screenshot below you can see that Peg highlighted Sep 3, 2015, when the Social Diva page garnered 15 new Likes.

Organic vs. Paid

"Organic reach" is the total number of unique people who were shown your post through unpaid distribution. "Paid reach" is the total number of unique people who were shown your post as a result of ads. In the example below it shows 15 Paid Likes on Sep 3, 2015.

Reach

Post reach is the number of people who've seen your post. (Your post counts as reaching someone when it's shown in their News Feed.)

As we click on to reach, you'll see both organic and paid reach; again, you can scroll over the chart to get specifics from a particular date. In the example below, there were 184 Organic Likes on Aug 31, 2015.

As you can see, on Sep 3, 2015, Peg's page got 246 Paid Likes. It's very easy to navigate around in this tool; you only need to move your mouse around to highlight events that happened on different dates.

Visits

"Visits" refers to the number of times your page was viewed. In this example, Page Visits, Info Tab and Photos Tab are displayed. Facebook Insights measures each area of the page and you can see the data easily here.

Posts

This screenshot shows a report on the performance of posts. In Peg's example, the report displays every post, including the image used, copy, type of post, and the post's targeting, reach, and engagement. This view makes it easy to get an overview of what's working and what isn't.

The "boost post" button is conveniently located in this view as well. Facebook makes it easy to boost the posts you want to have more visibility.

You can choose any post from the list and click on it for more detailed information. On the left. we have the post itself. On the right, you can see additional insights, such as the number of people reached, plus the number of Likes, comments, and shares. In Facebook's latest update, you can get a lot of this information right on your timeline. However, this data also lives here in the backend, providing a more focused approach that will likely be more useful in your workflow.

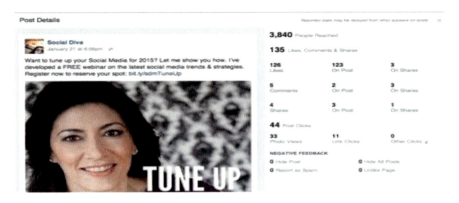

Video

In the Videos section of your Page Insights, you can see the following information about videos your Page has published or shared:

- The number of times videos were viewed.
- The number of times videos were viewed for 30 seconds or more.
- Your Page's most viewed videos.

To see Auto-Played vs. Clicked-to-Play or Unique vs. Repeat views, click Organic vs. Paid at the top-right of the chart, and then select the data you want to see.

People

The "People" tab is one of the most important tabs for you to regularly check, especially in the initial stages of setting up your Facebook page. This tab lets you get insights into the specific demographic characteristics of those that are following you. It's important to know whether these demographics actually match those of your ideal target audience. Hopefully there's a close match, but if not, you'll have to revisit your audience targeting settings and tweak them.

For example, In Peg's Social Diva page reporting example, it's no surprise to her that visitors to her Facebook page are largely women (87%), of medium (25-45) age, who mainly reside in New York City. That's the target market she's been working on, therefore this data validates that her Facebook marketing is on target and is working as intended.

That's great to know, but what's equally interesting is that Peg has some eyeballs coming from the European market. Perhaps Peg should think about whether she's got a product or service that might be appealing enough to promote specifically for the European market. This is the kind of data-driven insight that Peg might never have discovered on her own.

| | Overview | Likes | Reach | Visits | Posts | Videos | **People** |

Your Fans | People Reached | People Engaged

The people who like your Page

Women **87%** Your Fans
Men **12%** Your Fans

Age breakdown: 13-17: 0.307% / 0.0146%; 18-24: 4% / 0.993%; 25-34: 27% / 4%; 35-44: 32% / 4%; 45-54: 15% / 2%; 55-64: 5% / 0.815%; 65+: 3% / 0.424%

Country	Your Fans	City	Your Fans	Language	Your Fans
United States of America	5,993	New York, NY	1,594	English (US)	6,196
Canada	116	Brooklyn, NY	383	English (UK)	230
United Kingdom	63	Atlanta, GA	293	Spanish	130
Mexico	55	Los Angeles, CA	247	French (France)	42
Australia	41	Miami, FL	114	Spanish (Spain)	40
India	37	Chicago, IL	83	Portuguese (Brazil)	23
Romania	31	San Francisco, CA	76	Italian	21
France	29	Houston, TX	59	Romanian	16
Brazil	26	Washington, DC	50	Arabic	14
Pakistan	23	Bronx, NY	47	German	13
Argentina	20	San Diego, CA	41	Russian	11
Italy	18	Philadelphia, PA	37	Thai	11
Egypt	16	Dallas, TX	37	Indonesian	9
Germany	16	Queens, NY	37	Greek	7
Philippines	16	London, England, United ...	36	Turkish	7

The bottom line with Facebook Insights is it's a free and easy tool that lets you easily visualize your campaign's performance. If you've set things up correctly, chances are you won't have to spend too much time on it. But you should check it from time to time to make sure you're on track or, if you're not, so that you can pivot your Facebook marketing accordingly.

Reports

If you're really into data, you can export your reports for further analysis via Excel, Google Docs, or another spreadsheet program. You can use those reports to measure any kind of metrics you need to track and compute your ROI.

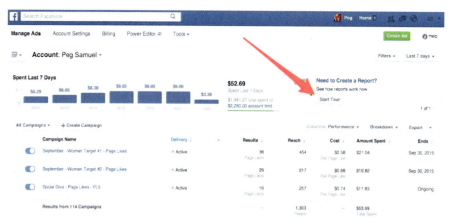

Key Takeaways

- Visit your Insights area on a regular basis
- Make sure you're hitting your target audience
- Observe how your posts are performing
- Use Reports on an ongoing basis to make sure Facebook is working for your business objectives
- Analyze Insights reports with an eye to discovering new markets

Facebook Like a Pro

If you've read and applied everything you've applied so far, you're no longer in the 95th percentile of social media marketers: you're in the 99th.

But don't pop the champagne yet. You'll still need to get better – and smarter – to compete against pro-level Facebook marketers. So let's turn our attention to some advanced techniques used by some of the best marketers on Facebook.

Advanced Facebook Tools for Brands

Want to market like the big guys? You can. Once you have some traction, let's talk about how to take your Facebook marketing to the ultimate level.

Measure like a Pro

Data is everything when it comes to digital. When you're a pro on Facebook, number crunching is "an inside job." What we mean here is you'll need to start analyzing metrics that go beyond Likes and demographics. By digging in and setting up metrics with greater insight, you can fine-tune your Facebook marketing tactics to gain the best ROI for your brand.

These social media analytics and publishing tools help the big guys and can help you too:

Social Bakers has a competitive comparison brand analysis feature that we love to use. You can upload other brands to see what and when they post. This is great information to have when building and scheduling your own content.

Simply Measured is one of the best tools on the market. It lets you understand the performance of your Facebook page in a bigger, more holistic way. You can set up reporting for amplification, reach, content, engagement trends, and even track the sentiment of each of your posts. Also, you can download easy to read and user-friendly reports straight to Powerpoint so they're ready to present to your team or investors.

Nuvi is a fantastic platform; their real time reporting is phenomenal. Peg's company worked with them on an influencer campaign that showed amplification of messaging from a high-influencer program and the reports were just stunning. In a nutshell, whenever an influencer would post about the campaign, the report would show in detail the impact of these messages as they went out across the web. Being able to show the client the massive impact of the overall campaign was just what was needed.

Sysomos is a power tool for brands and agencies that's driven by deep data; it's extremely helpful for measuring social ROI.

Sumall is a platform that combines social media, web traffic, sales metrics, and other data to allow customers to track business and social media metrics.

All of these tools are great, but in order to pick the one you're most comfortable with, consider the costs involved at the tier you require, request a demo, and be mindful of the amount of customer service you may need.

Power Editor

The Power Editor is an advanced tool in Facebook Ads. As of three months ago, it was the best place to duplicate campaigns, ad sets and add pixels to external pages.

However, with the launch of the new Ads Manager in August 2015, we wouldn't be surprised if Facebook consolidates its many tool options to just one.

Facebook Groups

A lot of marketers and communities are utilizing Facebook Groups because they offer a compelling way to garner even more engagement and conversation for your brand.

The sense of community and camaraderie within Groups can be pretty amazing. Most of what we see these groups being used for is internal support for business services or products. Groups are a highly engaging platform insofar as anyone and everyone in the group can post status updates, ask questions, and comment on any given post.

We think of Facebook Groups as multiple niche-based interest groups within Facebook where people from all over the world can connect and help with each other's goals/projects/ideas, and where business owners can nurture their paying customers.

For example, Peg has a Facebook Group organized around her online school. Anyone enrolled in the school is allowed access to this private group. (She keeps it private so when people ask questions, and enter conversations around her course material, these conversations will not be seen by anyone outside the group.) Having a private Group keeps the environment very similar to that in her classroom at New York University.

Plus, she's enabled a setting that only allows the owner or admins of the group to approve of a new member. Doing this ensures that the community is carefully managed and only paying students are exposed to questions regarding valuable course content.

Another great example is "PR, Marketing and Media Czars." This Facebook Group is highly engaged, helpful, and generous. Post content ranges from helping people to get products placed, to offering venues, to giving people a direct connection to celebrity agents. In PR, this is a valuable networking resource, because connecting with the right people is such a key success factor in that industry.

Pro Tip: If you're thinking about a Facebook Groups strategy, be mindful of what you're offering, your strategy behind it, and whether you have the internal resources necessary to manage it. Also, remember our main rule: "Less is More:" don't set up numerous Groups without having a clear strategy for each. Unmanaged, unengaged Facebook areas are nothing more than platforms for tumbleweeds.

Create content that demands attention

When you've arrived at the point that you have a super-engaged following, your page has been optimized, and your Facebook community has grown and matured, take a lesson from the big brands: be creative!

Change it up

When you start to see some energy around your content, change it up. Sometimes a long-form (blog type) post will garner a lot of attention. Sometimes five posts a day will create hype; sometimes you need to break out of the "standards" box and test new formulas according to what your business and brand represents. Test, trial, and experiment. And then experiment again – you might just create a new viral posting formula!

Facebook Success Stories

Let's look at some great brands for ideas. Some of these brands spend millions developing social media strategies. Observe and learn!

Gary Vaynerchuk #AskGaryVee

Gary has been a real influencer in the land of social media and it's no surprise he breaks through the clutter with his unique approach, which uses posts related to his 20-minute show, along with long-form content. This content mix works for Gary because his name is so widely known. He's extremely engaged with his community and is set up to pivot at any time in any direction!

Coca-Cola

With 92 million fans on Facebook, it's everyone's favorite brand play. They literally keep serving us up their same product in unique and fun ways. Most importantly, Coca-Cola really takes the time to engage with their audience. Coca-Cola's posts are simple, but its sparky digital approach provokes loads of fan engagement.

Zappos

A brand that's great on engagement and customer service. Besides being "social" and engaging, notice that when you engage, the post goes back into the News Feed, a point we made in an earlier chapter. It's free marketing!

Oreo

America's favorite cookie has taken its brand online so supremely. How creative do you think you could be with one cookie? They really do Facebook well. What is also extremely interesting is the engagement isn't just brand to customer, it's a conversation that invites all brand advocates: consumer-to-consumer, brand to consumer, consumer to brand. That's why the new wave of social media for business is so interesting.

Test, Measure, Pivot & Grow

Each of these brands has found a different cadence and format of posting that has worked well.

Some post less, some post more, some post long; some post short.

Our point is once you have some stickiness, start to think about your page the way the big brands think about theirs. Change things up, play with different approaches, "go with the flow" when that seems appropriate, and feel free to experiment.

Naturally, you'll want to test the results of your different creative approaches, to make sure you're not drifting too far from the core interests of your audience. Pivot towards what's working at any moment in time while still incorporating new ideas that flow from your audience.

Facebook Custom Audiences

Facebook Custom Audiences provide a way for you to leverage all the hard work you've done gathering email addresses over the years. For example, if you're selling any kinds of goods, you probably have e-mail addresses for all your customers, along with information on what they bought and how much they spent. Or you have lists of people who met you at trade shows, or downloaded your eBooks, subscribed to your online newsletter, or attended your online webinars.

Each of these lists can be used to generate unique audience on Facebook that you can market to with specific, highly personalized messaging. Generally, when marketers do this kind of interest-based hyper-targeting, they see better CTR rates, engagement, and other positive behavior such as brand lift.

Custom Audiences are relatively new, and while they've got great potential, a lot of marketers seem unaware of their existence. So learning about them and testing their effectiveness for you can give you a powerful jump on your competition.

Setting up a Custom Audience

The process for setting up a Custom Audience on Facebook is very simple.

You can use the Ad Manager or the Power Editor to do so (we'll use the Ad Manager in the example below).

Facebook provides three Custom Audiences options:

1. List-based Custom Audiences using email addresses, phone numbers, Facebook user IDs, or mobile advertiser IDs.

2. Website Traffic-based Custom Audiences that match visitors to your website with the IDs of Facebook users.

3. App Activity-based Custom Audiences that generate lists of people who've done specific things with people performing specific activities within apps, for example, when a player of a game reaches a certain goal in it.

Here's a step-by-step guide to setting up a List-based Custom Audience. (List-based audiences is the option that you'll probably use most often).

Step 1: Create Your Custom Audience

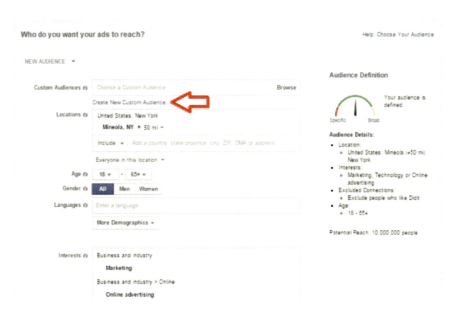

Go to Ads Manager, choose an objective (Boost your posts, Promote your page, etc.), and select the page you want this objective to apply to. Click on "Create Custom Audience" in the "Who Do You Want Your Ads to Reach?" area.

A "Create a Custom Audience" window will appear offering you three choices. The first choice is "Customer List," followed by "Website Traffic" and "App Activity." Choose "Customer List."

Step 2: Upload File

Now select "Upload a file." From here, you can upload (via file browsing or drag-and-drop) a list of names in either .csv or .txt format. Before doing so, select the type of data you're uploading (Emails, User IDs, phone numbers, or mobile advertiser IDs). Typically, you'll upload a .CSV file of the type used by spreadsheets such as Excel or Google Docs. You can also import your contacts directly from Mailchimp in this option.

Step 3: Check your formatting

Make sure that email addresses in your file are organized correctly. They should be in a single column of data with no heading.

For email lists, Facebook requires formatting like this:

name1@example.com
name2@example.com
name3@example.com

For phone numbers, Facebook requires formatting like this:
16505551234
16505551235

(No leading zeros from international country codes are permitted, nor are dashes in the number string.)

For mobile IDs, Facebook supports Android advertising IDs, Apple IDFA (Advertising Identifier) numbers, and Facebook App User IDs.

Best Practices

While creating Custom Audiences is easy, you'll need to plan carefully to get the most out of them. Here are some best practices to observe when using them:

1. Segment your lists before (not after) you upload them to Facebook

Once you upload your lists to Facebook, you won't be able to change their composition. That's why you need to think carefully in advance about how to segment your lists *before* you upload them.

For example, let's say you're an online merchant that sells mobile phone accessories. You've got a list of 1,000 people gathered from your CRM system. This list should be segmented very tightly, on the brand, product line, and perhaps even individual SKU level. Doing this will let you provide customized messaging on Facebook that's tailored to the specific qualities of each purchasing group.

Custom Audience lists can also be used to *exclude* certain people from being exposed to your ad campaigns. This feature can be very useful. For example, if your campaign is designed to attract new customers, you will not want to expose your existing customers to it.

2: Get real opt-in (don't scrape addresses)

You must make efforts to obtain true opt-ins from the human constituents of each list you upload. People who've signed up for your mailing list are such people; people whose addresses were "scraped" from websites, or otherwise have been added without their consent, are not!

Facebook's language on this policy is quite clear: you should abide by it:

You represent and warrant that you (or your data provider) have provided appropriate notice to and secured any necessary consent from the data subjects whose data will be hashed to create the Hashed Data, including as needed to be in compliance with all applicable laws, regulations and industry guidelines. If you have not collected the data directly from the data subject, you confirm, without limiting anything in these terms, that you have all necessary rights and permissions to use the data. If you are using a Facebook identifier to create a custom audience, you must have obtained the identifier directly from the data subject in compliance with these terms.

Source:
https://www.facebook.com/ads/manage/customaudiences/tos.php

Website Traffic-based Custom Audiences

Beyond list-based Custom Audiences, Facebook gives you a way to advertise to people on Facebook who've visited your website – and even specific pages of your website. You can create up to 10,000 Custom Audiences derived from your website visitors. That's a lot of power!

Website Traffic-based Custom Audiences are great for:

Remarketing to people on Facebook who've seen your site, are familiar with what you offer, but need a gentle "nudge" to convert.

Making your existing ads more efficient by *excluding* audiences of people who've already converted on your message or are undesirable for some other reason.

Creating "lookalike audiences" of people whose qualities are similar to those of people browsing your website

In the same way that you need to think carefully about segmenting your customer/prospect lists prior to uploading them to Facebook, you should plan how you want to segment your website visitors, because the characteristics – and value – of someone visiting your home page are going to be different from someone visiting a blog page, product page, or "about" page.

Each occupies a different stage in the "purchase funnel," after all, and should receive messages appropriate to this position. For example,

"**Early funnel**" people are those who probably aren't familiar with your brand. Message these people with ads that raise awareness of who you are.

"**Mid funnel**" people may have visited your Facebook business page, your website, or otherwise interacted with your brand online. But they're not yet convinced that they want to do business with you. Reach these people by explaining in more detail why you're a good choice.

"**Late funnel**" people know who you are, why you're good, and might just need a strategic nudge from you to become customers.

Facebook lets you define a different Custom Audience for visitors who move through the funnel on your web site. You can target people who:

1. Go to the home page of your site
2. Go to product category pages
3. Go to product-specific pages
4. Go to shopping cart pages
5. Go to "thank you pages" following shopping cart visits.

Using Custom Audiences lets you personalize your Facebook ad campaigns in a way that can be very effective by moving them through the conversion funnel. And right now, many marketers don't seem to be using this powerful method of reaching people on Facebook. We'd advise you to start testing Custom Audiences, both because they're effective and because using them may give you real "first mover advantage."

Who to Follow

Facebook is an ever-changing space filled with fancy algorithms, privacy rules, and new features that seem to come out of nowhere. That's Facebook's "technical side."

But Facebook is also filled with some very smart, very wise marketers who you should get to know personally. These folks pride themselves on sharing their hard-won business advice – advice that you might spend hundreds of dollars for if you paid to listen to them at an exclusive business conference – right on their Facebook business pages.

Here's a roundup of 12 of the best Facebook marketers. They all have Twitter presences as well. Friend them. Follow them. Pick their brains. (but please don't SPAM them).

@GuyKawasaki – Guy's mantra is "I empower people" and he's empowered thousands with his quirkily enthusiastic take on digital marketing. Currently, he's the "Chief evangelist of @Canva," Former chief evangelist of Apple, and championship Tweeter." If you can get his attention, and he happens to retweet something you've written or posted, expect a flood of traffic.

@MariSmith – Mari has helped many – from big luxury brands to entrepreneurs like yourself – master marketing on Facebook and Instagram. Get to know Mari – and study closely how she markets herself on and off Facebook, because she's a true pro at the game.

@DaveKerpen – Dave's a best-selling author and top-tier columnist who's thought long and hard about building "Likeable" businesses. His Twitter and Facebook feeds are filled with high-quality, timely content. Read what he writes and emulate his approach!

@PegFitzpatrick – Peg Fitzgerald ("Rockin' a positive attitude") is another person who really "gets" social media. Her feed – friendly, casual, and thoughtful – is filled with tips you can quickly apply to get better results from your own social media efforts.

@garyvee – Gary Vaynerchuck ("Family 1st! but after that, Businessman.") is a pioneer of what's now called "influencer marketing."

When Gary's not addressing big crowds at conferencing, he's busy producing a lively feed with lots of great strategies and tactics you can employ in your social media marketing.

@jonloomer – John Loomer covers the fast-changing developments in Facebook marketing very closely. His feed is a great place to learn about the latest Facebook tool or growth hack.

@ravishukle – Ravi Shukle dubs himself a "Guardian of Consumer Happiness" whose focus is on bringing CRM (Customer Relationship Management) and social media together. His feed is a great place to learn about social media's growing role in CRM.

@Mike_Stelzner – Mike's the founder of the popular Social Media Examiner website, which means he's 100 percent up on the latest social trends. He also runs a popular and entertaining podcast on social media you should check out.

@JasonFalls – Jason Falls is up on all the latest trends in social media, content marketing, and inbound marketing, and his feeds are funny and wise to boot.

@bsainsbury – Bonnie Sainsbury has a lot to say about web design, social media, and conversions. She takes special pride in demystifying complicated marketing jargon to make today's marketing technologies more accessible to humans.

@AndreaVahl – Andrea Vahl's feeds are chock-ablock with strategic and tactical tips for budding social media marketing stars. She's also a wickedly witty writer.

@jeremarketer - Jeremy Goldman (who so kindly wrote the Foreword to this book) is a thought leader in the social space. His feeds are mixed with humor and wisdom, making him one of our favorite people to follow.

And of course don't forget to follow us at **@SocialDiva** and **@SearchDecoder**

If you want to step up your Facebook game, follow everyone on this list. The content they share on a daily basis is a never-ending fountain of useful knowledge!

Bonus

You've reached the end of our book, and we hope we've left you stronger, wiser, and better equipped to move your brand and your business forward on Facebook. But we didn't want to leave you without giving you this bonus chapter about Instagram, because it's lately become a powerful tool for visual branding and fan acquisition, and it's likely that its features will become more tightly integrated with Facebook in the future (because, of course, Facebook now owns Instagram).

Like I'm 5 Guide to Instagram

What does photo app service Instagram have to do with Facebook? Well, back in 2014 Facebook acquired Instagram for $1 billion. Instagram is a social, visual platform that focuses on captivating imagery. It gives you an opportunity to tell your brand's story in a way that no other social media channel provides.

Currently, Instagram has over 300 million active monthly users and a growing army of brands is taking advantage of the platform to share their distinctive points of view.

Here are some tips for optimizing your Instagram presence:

Keep things consistent

Keep your branding consistent across all social media platforms. Choose an account name that appropriately represents your business name. Try not to use numbers or other characters that might deter your customers from finding you.

Your profile photo – like your account name – should be readily recognizable and visually synonymous with your brand. Keep it simple: perhaps a logo or your headshot (if you represent a personal brand). Image dimensions should be 150×150 pixels. (Using the same image you selected for your Facebook Icon works perfectly).

Make sure your Instagram Bio is filled out and reads professionally. Make sure that you also include the URL to your website. (Ideally, the data in this area will be identical to that in your Facebook Bio area).

Let's talk photos

Your photos should be of very high quality; they should feel creative, and "instantaneous." Because Instagram is a visual platform, make sure your pictures are interesting, in-focus and have good lighting. Lighting is really key here: we've seen many photos that miss the mark because they're badly lit.

You don't have to be a professional photographer to create good-looking images for Instagram. There's no doubt that having a background in photography basics – especially composition – will help you create better images. But Instagram gives you many tools to fix up your images prior to posting.

Photo tricks

Here are a couple of photo tips to consider:

- Newer smart phones (right now, iPhone 6 and newer) are perfect for creating, editing, and enhancing Instagram images.
- When you're about to snap a shot, hold elbows in to keep your phone steady.
- Tap center of screen for clarity.
- Brightness: the Instagram App has a sun icon you can tap to brighten your image (you can also brighten up the image from the phone app as well).
- Filters: Instagram has many filters you can use to change the color and lightness of the photo. It's OK to play with these filters, but don't go overboard: try to stick with one so that your images have a consistent look.
- Instagram has a "one-button" tool that adjusts everything (brightness, contrast, structure, saturation) that's very handy.

Instagram Content

Use Instagram to tell your brand story. Use your brand colors, be mindful of what your brand is about, and think about how you want to visually feature it. Be consistent and strive for a high level of quality: remember: before people decide whether to follow you. They'll typically look at the full layout of your account.

Need content ideas?

Naturally, all of your Instagram content needs to support your brand's visual identity. But you can still experiment with many different kinds of posts and content types. Here are some to consider:

- "Behind the scenes," insider-style visual content
- Physical products, if you can show them in an interesting way
- Lifestyle images
- Images of your physical location. People like to know that you're real and live in a real place. Pull images that do this into your feed
- #THT or Throw Back Thursday-style posts. Use these to highlight brand relevant images from the past
- Aspirational posts
- "Flat Lays." These are very popular right now, see example below

Create amplifying captions. Besides having a great photo, use a caption that enhances it. The caption is also a great place to bring in your brand's story in a natural way.

Check out this example on Peg's Instagram feed:

You can see how she brought both her work life and brand into this shot.

Be unique. Keep what you post relevant to your authentic voice, or – if you are a business – always include some aspect of your brand story. Remember: you are an individual unlike any other! Bring that sense of uniqueness to your social media posts.

How often should I post?

Posting rules for Instagram are very similar to those of Facebook. Be consistent (but remember: less is always more). Post regularly (1-2 posts per day is best practice) but if you don't have quality content, post less (or not at all).

Pro tip: Spare the world the "4 photo ambush" posts that come all at once — it's the fastest way to annoy people and thus lose followers. Remember: Quality always trumps Quantity.

Should I connect Instagram to Facebook?

Yes! You can connect your Instagram presence to your Facebook presence. You do this in the Settings area of your Instagram account. But if you do this, make sure you keep both feeds professional (e.g. are those cute pictures of your kids/dogs/friends kittens really relevant?). After connecting your accounts, head back to Facebook and clean up any @ or # symbols that might have cropped up in the connection process. Your Facebook page should always look clean, sharp and active.

What are #'s all about?

Hashtags make content searchable on Instagram. Use hashtags to increase organic visibility. Don't overuse them, however. Do some searches for the hashtags most relevant to your brand. The best way to use them is to put them in the first "comment," therefore keeping your caption clean and easy to read.

Schedule it!

Did you know you can schedule your Instagram posts? (This was the best news we had heard in awhile!) You can use ScheduGram (http://schedugr.am/) to do this. The tool can make managing one – or multiple – Instagram accounts a lot easier. It includes editing tools, bulk uploads, and provides for multiple users (if you're managing more than one account this can be a real life-saver).

Engage and build your following

Instagram – like Facebook – is SOCIAL media, which means you must engage. Engage with your followers, Likers, and other accounts relevant to the business you're in.

Make sure you:

- Like others' photos
- Comment on others' photos
- Include #
- Comment back to people who are commenting on your photos. Make sure you use the @ sign to tag them back so they are notified.
- Regram photos you like #regram or (camera emoji) You can Regram fan photos and relevant images. Doing this will increase fan engagement and photo diversity in your feed. Make sure you tag/credit the original post owner's handle.

Tip: take a screenshot and then re-post (as opposed to using a regram app). It's far more visually appealing when viewed using Instagram's "tile" view).

Market yourself

Top Instagrammers know how to market themselves. They observe all the best practices, take great photos, and maintain great looking feeds, but they also know that this is only half the battle. Sure, you need your Instagram feed to be visually excellent. But you also have to raise its banner high on your other marketing channels.

Market yourself by doing the following:

- Add an Instagram icon to your website
- Tell your email list all about your great visual feed
- If you do any public speaking, or TV, mention your Instagram feed
- Tell people and list your Instagram feed address on your business card

Final Takeaways

- Ensure your account is professional (looks and reads well)
- Make great photos
- Tell your brand story
- Create authentic, valuable content
- Create amplifying captions
- Post consistently, but remember, Quality always trumps Quantity
- Use Hashtags
- Schedule
- Engage
- Market yourself

About the Authors

Peg Samuel

Peg Samuel, Adjunct Professor at New York University and Founder of Social Diva Media; she is a proven leader in online brand building and digital strategy. With twenty years experience in the digital marketing arena, Peg turned her love of communications into a lucrative and insight-driven Social Media consultancy specializing in social media strategy, brand influencer campaigns, and execution marketing for lifestyle, luxury, and high-profile celebrity brands.

Peg has worked with media brands including W Hotels, Harper's Bazaar, InStyle, and Vogue. Other special projects include the NBC Olympics Games (known as the first "Social" Olympics), the 55th Annual GRAMMY Awards, and the New Music Seminar. Peg is a sought after speaker, she has been on panels and given talks at Social Media Week, WIX, Social Media Breakfast, Internet Week New York, and Digital Hollywood.

Peg is the author of "*How to be a Social Diva*;" she's also produced two music albums with International House's music label, Strictly Rhythm: "Strictly Social Diva." She has received attention from E! News, MSNBC, Entrepreneur Magazine, and Good Morning New York. Her social networking contact base reads like a Who's Who in the entertainment, media, and advertising industries.

Useful Links:
Website: http://socialdivamedia.com/
Facebook: https://www.facebook.com/socialdiva
Twitter: https://twitter.com/socialdiva

Matthew Capala

Matthew Capala is the President of Alphametic, an organic growth accelerator specializing in SEO and social media workshops and consulting, with a portfolio of worldwide brands including L'Oreal, Hoval, and Quest Diagnostics. As a prolific Internet entrepreneur, Matthew has built several popular blogs, including Search Decoder and Sumo Hacks. He is a sought-after International speaker and trainer.

His work and ideas have been recognized by Mashable, Chicago Tribune, and The Huffington Post. As Adjunct Professor at NYU, Matthew teaches a course on search marketing and social media analytics. He writes regularly on The Next Web and is the author of four books, including "*SEO Like I'm 5: The Ultimate Beginner's Guide to Search Engine Optimization*."

With over a decade of digital marketing experience working with some of the world's largest brands (Apple, Western Union, Smirnoff, Dell, LG, and Prudential) and emerging startups, Matthew has leveraged the Internet in unprecedented ways to spur growth. Formerly Head of Search and Inbound Marketing (the Americas) at Profero (later acquired by Lowe & Partners), Matthew has built a million-dollar business, growing the group from one to nine in less than two years. Former leadership positions include specialist roles at Mindshare, Mediacom, Zeta Interactive, Mattel, and The Associated Press.

Useful links:
Website: http://alphametic.com/
SEO Blog: http://www.searchdecoder.com/
Life Hacking Blog: http://sumohacks.com/
FB: https://www.facebook.com/matt.capala/
Twitter: https://twitter.com/SearchDecoder

Other Books by the Authors

Peg Samuel

How to Be a Social Diva, An Essential Guide for the Girl About Town

Matthew Capala

SEO Like I'm 5: The Ultimate Beginner's Guide to Search Engine Optimization

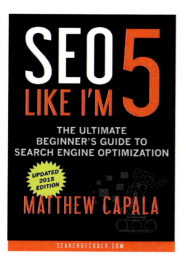

Soloprenuer Ronin: Break the Chains, Earn Your Freedom, and Engineer a Happy Internet Lifestyle Blogging From Anywhere

99 SEO Tools for 99 Cents (Kindle Only)

Made in the USA
Coppell, TX
09 May 2022

77596266R00088